Frightfully Fun

HALLOWEEN

Crafts & Cooking

Publications International, Ltd.
Favorite Brand Name Recipes at www.fbnr.com

Pictured on front cover *(clockwise from top left)*: Ghost on a Stick *(page 106)*; Friendly Witch *(page 12)*; Scarecrow Cupcakes *(page 120)*; Spooky Tic-Tac-Toe *(page 58)*.

Pictured on back cover *(clockwise from top left)*: Witchy Woman *(page 50)*; Mummy Dogs *(page 68)*.

Manufactured in China.

8 7 6 5 4 3 2 1

ISBN: 0-7853-5802-1

Microwave Cooking: Microwave ovens vary in wattage. Use the cooking times as guidelines and check for doneness before adding more time.

Preparation/Cooking Times: Preparation times are based on the approximate amount of time required to assemble the recipe before cooking, baking, chilling, or serving. These times include preparation steps such as measuring, chopping, and mixing. The fact that some preparations and cooking can be done simultaneously is taken into account. Preparation of optional ingredients and serving suggestions is not included.

Contents

FOREWORD TO FEAR

These wickedly wonderful crafts and devilishly delicious delights bring treats and people together in the spirit of Halloween.

While most of the activities in this book were created for big witches and warlocks, little goblins are always welcome to participate—and one chapter is designed specifically for them. Before you begin your reign of terror, please read below.

Each project and recipe includes a list of materials or ingredients as well as photos and step-by-step instructions. Take the time to go over the instructions carefully, and make sure you've got everything on hand before you throw anything into the witches' brew. It is a good idea to cover your work area with newspaper before beginning any project.

Be certain to keep a watchful eye on kids. You should read each project in the Spirited Kids' Projects chapter before deciding whether the project requires adult supervision. When making your decision, pay extra attention in the materials lists to items that are small, like beads, and items that can be hot, like an oven or a glue gun. If the child has never used a glue gun, explain that both the nozzle and freshly applied glue are hot. Have a glass of water nearby just in case warm fingers need cooling. Also, if kids paint with acrylic paints, have them wear an apron, because after the paint dries, it is permanent. If paint does get on their clothes, wash with soap and warm water immediately.

GENERAL PATTERN INSTRUCTIONS

When a project's instructions tell you to cut out a shape according to the pattern, trace the pattern from the book onto tracing paper, using a pencil. If the pattern has an arrow with the word *FOLD* next to a line, it is a half pattern. Fold a sheet of tracing paper in half, and open the paper. Place the fold line of the tracing paper exactly on top of the fold line of the pattern, and trace the pattern with a pencil. Then refold and cut along the line, going through both layers. Open the paper for the full pattern.

Some patterns in this book are printed smaller than actual size. You should enlarge them on a photocopier before using them, copying the pattern at the percentage indicated near the pattern.

PAINTS AND SUPPLIES

Paints

Acrylic paint dries in minutes, and cleanup is easy with soap and water. Many brands of acrylic paint are available at local stores. You can choose your favorite colors regardless of brand.

Finishes

Varnishes to protect your finished projects are available in both spray and brush-on. Brush-on water-base varnish dries in minutes and cleans up with soap and water. Use it over any acrylic paint. Spray varnish can be used over any type of paint or medium. For projects with a pure white surface, choose a nonyellowing varnish. The slight yellowing of some varnishes can actually enhance certain colors for a richer look. Varnishes are available in matte, satin, and gloss finishes. Choose the shine you prefer. Be sure to work in a well-ventilated area when using varnishes.

Brushes

Foam (sponge) brushes work well for sealing, base-coating, and varnishing wood. They can be cleaned with soap and water.

Synthetic brushes work well with acrylic paints for details and designs. Use a liner brush for thin lines and details. An angle brush is used to fill large areas and to float (or side-load) color (see next page). A large flat brush is used to apply base coat and varnish. Small flat brushes are for stroke work and base-coating small areas.

BASIC PAINTING TECHNIQUES

Thin lines

1 Thin paint with 50 percent water for a fluid consistency that flows easily off the brush.

2 Use a liner brush for short lines and tiny details. Dip brush into thinned paint. Wipe excess on palette.

3 Hold brush upright. Use your little finger as a balance when painting. For extra-thin lines, don't apply pressure.

Step 3

Floating (or side-loading) color

This technique is used to shade or highlight the edge of an object. It is a gradual blend of color to water.

1 Moisten an angle brush with water. Blot excess water from brush, setting bristles on paper towel until shine of water disappears.

2 Dilute thicker paint with 50 percent water. Dip the long corner of the brush into paint. Load paint sparingly. Carefully stroke the brush on your palette until the color blends halfway across the brush. If the paint blends all the way to the short side, clean the brush and load again.

3 Hold the brush at a 45-degree angle, and using a light touch, apply color to designated area.

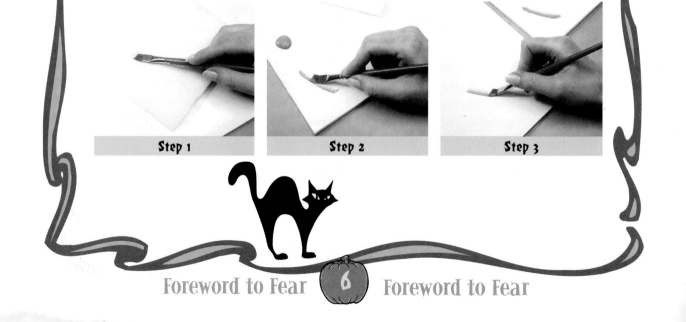

Step 1   **Step 2**   **Step 3**

MAKING A BOW

1 Unroll several yards from a bolt of ribbon. Form loops from the ribbon with your dominant hand. Pinch the center of the loops with the thumb and forefinger of your other hand as you work.

2 Continue to add loops to your bow. Keep pinching the bow's center with your thumb and forefinger. After you have all the loops you want, trim away excess ribbon from the bolt. If you want a streamer, leave the ribbon longer before cutting.

3 Insert a length of wire through the center of the ribbon. Bring the two wire ends securely and tightly next to the bow's center to eliminate loop slippage. Attach the bow with the wire. You may also trim the wire and glue the bow in place.

Step 1   Step 2   Step 3

Note: When using heavier ribbon, use a chenille stem to secure the bow. The tiny hairs on the stem will hold the bow securely and not allow potential twisting of the bare wire. For tiny, delicate bows, thin cloth-covered wire can be used for securing. It eliminates slipping and is so tiny that it disappears into the bow loops.

It's a good idea to make each activity following the instructions exactly. Then feel free to create another, using your imagination, adding ingredients or changing colors, making it even more yours. Think of all the variations you can make and how much you'll have to share!

Most important, have a frighteningly fun time! You'll be proud to say, "I made this myself!"

Junior and His Mummy

Wind some thrills and
shrills around these mummies.
They're sure to provide a
RIP-roaring time.

WHAT YOU'LL NEED

Small and large clothespin
   dolls

Tacky glue

Muslin: two 4×3-inch pieces
   and two 3¼×2½-inch pieces
   (optional)

Ruler

Sewing machine and white
   thread (optional)

Polyester fiberfill (optional)

Low-temp glue gun (optional)

Glue sticks (optional)

White acrylic paint

Paintbrush

3 yards cheesecloth

Scissors

2 comical plastic eyes,
   12.5mm each

1 yard black satin ribbon,
   $\frac{1}{16}$ inch wide

Miniature fall leaves

Miniature pumpkin

Miniature pumpkin treat bag

Flocked bat

1 Assemble clothespin dolls. For fabric arms, fold 3¼×2½-inch muslin pieces to measure 3¼×1¼ inches. Sew along short end and length with ¼-inch seam allowance. Turn arms and stuff firmly with fiberfill, leaving ¼ inch at opening. Working with one arm at a time, apply low-temp glue to shoulder of doll. Press raw edges of arm into wood. Arm should be secure and stand straight out from side of body. Repeat for all arms. Let glue set.

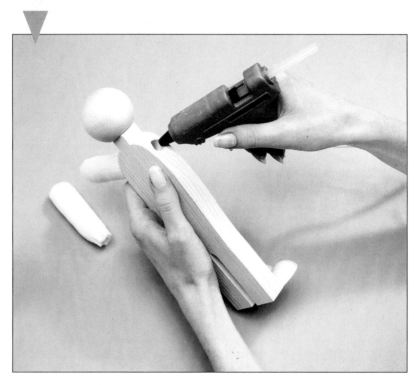

2 Paint entire doll with white paint. Apply second coat of white if needed. Let dry.

3 Cut cheesecloth into 1-inch-wide strips. Starting with large mummy, apply a line of tacky glue along bottom edge of body. Place a strip of cheesecloth on top of glue. Press cloth into wood. Trim excess cloth from bottom. Starting at back of body, place a small amount of glue on one leg. Attach one end of strip to glue and wrap around leg, ending at top of leg. Secure end of strip with glue. Repeat for other leg. Continue wrapping strips of cheesecloth around body and arms. Start and end at back, slightly overlapping strips. At head, apply crossing lines of glue. Place strips across head.

While wrapping, allow some pieces to hang about 2 to 4 inches from mummy at body, arm, and head. Twist cloth gently. Repeat to wrap Junior.

4 Remove shanks from eyes. Glue eyes to mummies. Make a simple bow with black ribbon and glue to large mummy. Glue leaves and pumpkin to large mummy hand. Glue pumpkin treat bag to Junior's arm. Glue flocked bat to Junior's body at front.

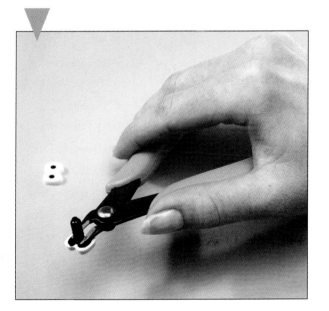

Friendly Witch

This friendly witch will last a lot longer than the sweet treats!

WHAT YOU'LL NEED

- 18-inch premade muslin doll
- Green acrylic paint
- Paintbrush
- Red fine-tipped permanent marker
- Powder blush makeup
- Scissors
- ½ yard black broadcloth
- Sewing machine and black thread
- Needle and thread
- 5 star buttons
- 2 moon/star buttons
- ½ yard Halloween print fabric
- Iron
- 24 inches black ribbon, ¹⁄₁₆ inch wide
- Tacky glue
- 6-inch black felt witch hat
- 12 inches satin orange ribbon, ¾ inch wide
- Waxed paper
- Glow-in-the-dark dimensional paint: orange, yellow
- Skein orange yarn
- 12×4-inch cardboard hair template

1 Paint 2 green dots on doll face for eyes. Draw smile with permanent red marker. Let dry. Brush on cheeks with powder blush. Apply blush lightly until satisfied with color.

2 Enlarge pattern on page 154 200 percent (see page 4 for instructions). Cut black broadcloth in half. Using pattern, fold one broadcloth piece on *FOLD* line and cut. Repeat with other broadcloth piece. Slit along solid fold line. Following pattern instructions, sew with ¼-inch seam allowance. Clip corners and turn romper right side out. Slip romper on doll through neck opening. Turn raw edges of neckline down ¼ inch and sew a running stitch around neckline. Knot off.

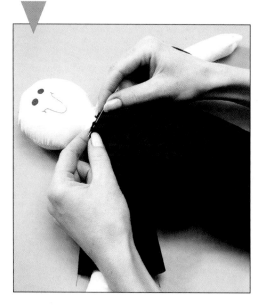

3 Turn sleeves under ¼ inch and gather with running stitch. Gather at doll's elbow and knot off. Turn pant hems under ¼ inch and gather with running stitch. Gather at ankle and knot off.

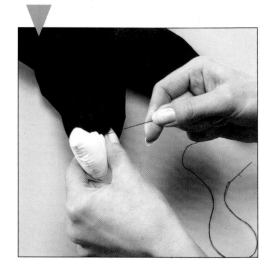

4 Center 3 star buttons on front of romper, and sew them to romper. First button is ½ inch from top of neckline, and buttons are spaced 1 inch apart. Sew moon/star buttons to outside bottom of romper legs.

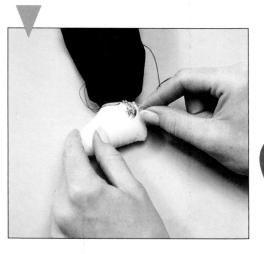

5 Sew side and bottom seams on cape (use Halloween print). Fold top raw edge of cape down 1 inch (wrong sides together) and iron crease. Sew a running stitch across cape 1 inch down from top. Gather to neckline. Place cape on doll. To measure, pull gathers until ends surround face, but don't cover face. Knot off. Sew last 2 star buttons to cape. Cut black ribbon into three 8-inch pieces. Glue ribbons to inside of cape, even with star buttons. Allow glue to set.

6 Wrap orange ribbon around base of hat. Tie ribbon into simple bow. Trim ribbon. Tack ribbon to hat with a small amount of glue.

7 With leftover black material, cut 2 pieces of fabric 6×7 inches. Place 1 piece on waxed paper. Write "Trick or Treat" on fabric with orange glow-in-the-dark paint. Dot yellow glow-in-the-dark paint around writing. Allow paint to dry 24 hours. Fold tops of fabric down 1 inch. With right sides together, sew bag together with ¼-inch seam allowance. Turn bag. Glue last piece of 8-inch ribbon to bag for handle.

8 Wrap yarn around a 12-inch hair template about 20 times (depends on how thick yarn is). Cut one end of yarn from template. Remove three strands. Find center of hair and use a yarn strand to tie a temporary knot at center. Measure 3¼ inches down from center and tie a permanent knot. Repeat for other side. Remove temporary knot. Apply a thin line of glue across top of doll's head. Slightly twist hair between permanent knots, place hair over glue, and hold in place. Make sure ponytails are balanced on doll's head. Once glue has set, tack hair to doll with needle and thread and knot off. If hair doesn't seem secure, apply more glue under hair line and hold in place until glue sets.

Halloween Wreath

This friendly cat welcomes Halloween with its own wreath.

WHAT YOU'LL NEED

Tracing paper

Pencil

Cold-press watercolor paper, 300#

Scissors

Craft knife

Acrylic paint: snow white, dove gray, shading flesh, buttermilk, pumpkin, ebony black, mint julep, red iron oxide, cadmium yellow, light avocado

Paintbrushes: #2 flat, ³⁄₈-inch angle, 10/0 liner

Acrylic matte-finish spray

Grapevine wreath, medium size

3 yards ribbon, ¾ inch wide

24 inches ribbon, ⅛ inch wide

1 Trace pattern on page 152 and transfer to watercolor paper. Use scissors to cut out basic shape; clean cut corners and cut holes for ties with craft knife.

2 Use flat brush to base-coat the sign with snow white paint. Base-coat cat with dove gray and cat nose with shading flesh. Base-coat background under cat with buttermilk. Base-coat pumpkin with pumpkin paint and base-coat pumpkin eyes and mouth with ebony black. Base-coat pumpkin stem and leaves with mint julep. Allow to dry. Apply detail to pattern.

3 Contour pumpkin ridges by floating with red iron oxide (see page 6 for additional information on floating color). Float the dimensions of pumpkin face with cadmium yellow. Float stem and leaves with light avocado. Float contours of cat with ebony black and line features with ebony black.

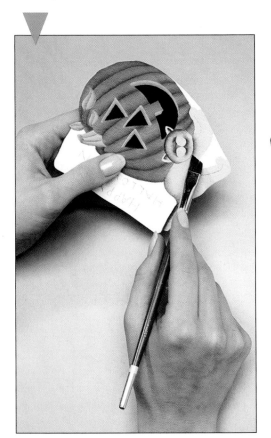

4 Use liner brush to line pumpkin with ebony black. Paint "HAPPY HALLOWEEN" with ebony black and add dots. Paint vine with light avocado. Allow to dry. Spray with acrylic matte-finish spray.

5 Wrap ¾-inch-wide ribbon around wreath and tie in a decorative bow (see page 7). Thread ⅛×24-inch piece of ribbon through tie holes in the ornament so that free ends are at the back. Tie ornament to wreath.

Jack-O'-Lantern

This floral piece will delight the hearts of young and old.

WHAT YOU'LL NEED

7-inch terra cotta jack-o'-lantern or 7-inch terra cotta container

Black acrylic paint (optional)

Paintbrush (optional)

3×5-inch piece dry foam

Hot glue gun

Glue sticks

Handful Spanish moss

Greening pins

9 pieces dried rust-colored wheat

Scissors

3 stems dried dock

3 stems dried strawflowers

1 twig dried bronze canella

2 stems preserved brown oak leaves

1 stem dried love grass

1 stem dried protea green

4 strings peach raffia ribbon

Florist wire

1 If using a plain terra cotta container, paint a jack-o'-lantern face with black acrylic paint. Let dry.

2 Glue the dry foam to the inverted hat of the jack-o'-lantern. Set the inverted hat on top of the pumpkin head, and moss lightly. Secure the moss with greening pins. Cut the rust-colored wheat in half, and insert each half horizontally into the sides of the foam.

3 Place the dock vertically in the center of the arrangement. Add the strawflowers from the base of the hat and work upward. Place the bronze canella in the lower right corner, allowing it to cascade downward. Fill in with brown oak leaves, love grass, and protea green as desired.

4 Make a bow from the raffia (see page 7), and attach it to the right side of the jack-o'-lantern with wire.

Halloween Button Covers

Have horrific fun making these fashionable button covers.

WHAT YOU'LL NEED

Tracing paper

Pencil

Cardboard

Scissors

White, black, and orange fabric scraps

Fusible webbing

Iron and ironing board

Press-and-peel foil kit (kit contains foil, dimensional bond, foil sealer, and applicator brush)

Button covers

Hot glue gun

Glue sticks

Buttons

Needle and thread

1 Using patterns on page 153, trace shapes onto cardboard and cut out. Set aside.

2 Following manufacturer's instructions, iron fusible webbing to fabric.

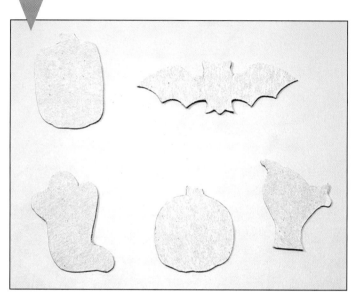

3 Trace a front and back for each cardboard shape onto fused fabric, then cut out.

4 Fuse fabric shapes onto front and back of cardboard cutouts from Step 1. Trim any excess fabric or cardboard from edges.

5 Following manufacturer's directions in press-and-peel kit, outline edges of shapes and draw in details using dimensional bond. Let dry until clear. Apply foil by rubbing firmly over dimensional bond with finger. Peel back excess foil from top. Edges and details of shapes should be covered by foil.

6 Glue button covers to back of each shape using hot glue gun. Press down on button cover to secure firmly.

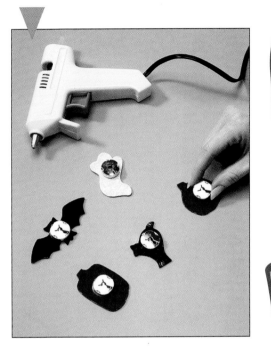

7 Sew buttons to favorite suspenders or shirt, and fasten button covers to the buttons.

Henrietta Witch

Henrietta is a nice witch, sure to delight all the little ghosts and goblins.

WHAT YOU'LL NEED

- ¼ yard unbleached muslin
- 1 package tan dye
- Tracing paper
- Pencil
- Cardboard or plastic
- Scissors
- Water-erasable marker or fabric-marking pencil
- Pins
- Sewing machine
- Cream thread
- Needle
- 10 ounces polyester fiberfill
- ¼ yard each brown-and-black check, brown plaid, and black fabrics
- 2 small black beads
- 10 inches red embroidery floss
- Powder blush makeup
- 1 ounce wool roving
- Craft glue
- ½ yard black ribbon, ⅛ inch wide
- 1½×4-inch piece gold-brown fabric
- Wooden meat skewer

1 Wash and dry muslin. Do not use fabric softener. Following manufacturer's directions, dye muslin in sink.

2 Enlage patterns from page 157 200 percent (see page 5 for instructions). Trace onto cardboard or plastic and cut out. Leg-shoe is one piece, and seam line is marked.

3 With muslin folded (9×22 inches), trace arms and head-body, leaving ½ inch between pieces. Traced lines are seam lines. Cut around all pieces ¼ inch away from seam lines.

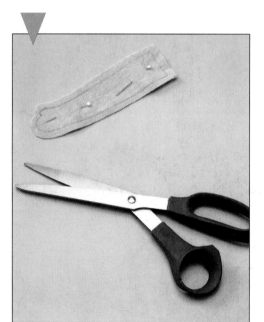

4 Stitch around arms, leaving top open. Clip curves and turn right side out. Stuff with polyester fiberfill to 1 inch below top. Baste top closed.

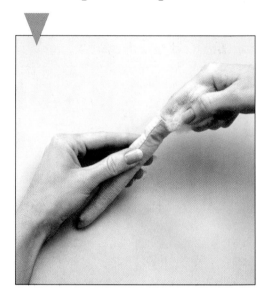

5 Stitch from A to B around head. Pin arms in place at sides. Stitch sides, catching arms in seams. Clip curves and turn right side out.

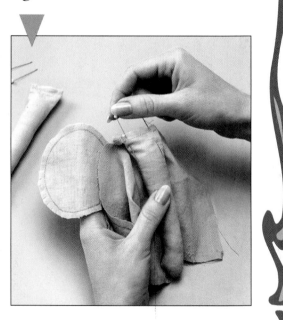

6 Cut 2½×15-inch piece from black fabric; cut 9×15-inch piece from muslin. Stitch pieces together along 15-inch side and press seam toward black fabric. On wrong side of doubled fabric, trace leg-shoe twice, lining up seam line with seam. (Remember to leave ½ inch between pieces.) Cut out leg-shoe ¼ inch from traced lines.

7 Stitch around leg-shoe on traced lines, leaving top open. Clip curves and turn right side out. Stuff with polyester fiberfill to 1¼ inches below top. Place seams side by side and baste across the top.

8 Stitch legs to front body at opening, making sure feet are forward. Stuff head and body with fiberfill, and stitch opening closed.

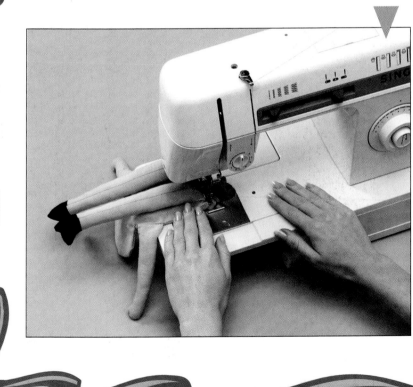

9 Pinch face together to form nose and take 2 stitches through pinched fabric and fiberfill. Stitch on small black beads for eyes. With red floss, embroider mouth. Using finger, put blush on cheeks.

10 Trace and cut out dress and sleeves from check fabric, vest from plaid, and hat from black.

11 Stitch dress at shoulder seams, and stitch sleeves to dress. Fringe bottom of sleeves by cutting slits 1 inch deep and ¼ inch apart. Stitch sleeve and side seams. Fringe bottom of dress in the same manner as sleeves. Hem neck opening. Place dress on doll and gather at neck and sleeves above fringe.

12 Cut front vest at fold line. Hem vest armholes, neck, front, and bottom. Stitch shoulder seams. Place vest on doll.

13 Using craft glue, glue wool roving on doll to form hair. Use fingers to lightly comb hair. Stitch back seam on hat and turn right side out. Turn brim of hat up in front and glue in place. Glue hat on doll's head. Tie black ribbon into a bow and glue to front neck of dress.

14 Fringe gold-brown fabric in same manner as sleeves. Glue to end of meat skewer. Roll fabric around bottom of skewer, gluing as you roll to form broom. Stitch broom to hands at thumbs.

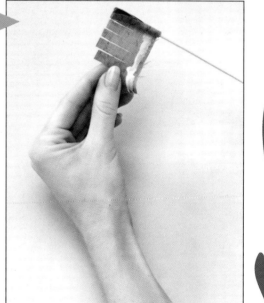

Welcome Placard

Welcome ghosts and goblins, bogeymen, and witches with this plaque.

WHAT YOU'LL NEED

8×13½-inch oval wood plaque
Fine sandpaper, #200
Tack cloth
Wood sealer
Paintbrushes: Foam or 1-inch flat, small flat, ½-inch flat, ⅜-inch angle, 10/0 liner

Acrylic paints: ebony black, dove gray, pumpkin, snow white, flesh tone, raw sienna, avocado, burnt orange, light cinnamon, gooseberry pink
Tracing paper
Pencil
Acrylic matte spray

1 Sand wood with fine sandpaper and use tack cloth to remove dust. Apply wood sealer to outer edge of plaque with a foam or 1-inch flat brush. Let dry. Paint outer edge with ebony black using small flat brush, and paint plaque with dove gray using ½-inch flat brush. Let dry. Enlarge pattern (on page 153) 130 percent, and apply basic outlines of pattern (just shapes) to plaque using tracing paper and pencil.

2 Using the small flat paintbrush, paint pumpkin costume and small pumpkin with pumpkin; treat bag and ghost costume with snow white; skin with flesh tone; hair with raw sienna; leaf and legs with avocado; and pumpkin faces, ghost's eyes and shoes, child's eyes, and handles with ebony black.

3 Apply detail pattern lines to plaque. Float a shade with angle brush (see instructions on page 6): shade pumpkins with burnt orange; skin with light cinnamon; ghost, ghost's shoes, and treat bag with dove gray; leaf, legs, and floor with ebony black; and child's cheeks with gooseberry pink.

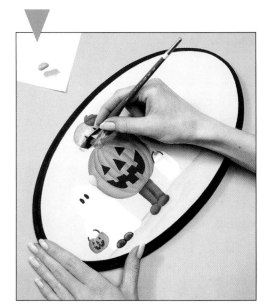

4 Using 10/0 liner brush, line hair with light cinnamon. Line shapes and bows with ebony black.

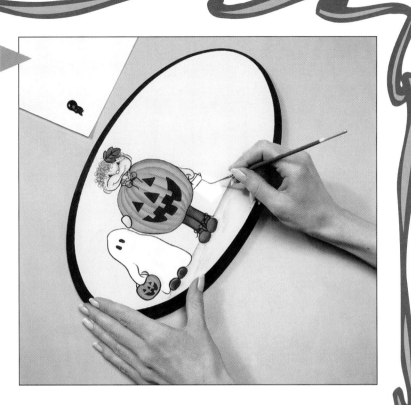

5 Apply pattern for words and line with ebony black. Apply letter dots with ebony black using the wooden end of paintbrush, redipping in paint for each dot. Finish by spraying with acrylic matte spray.

Spooky Skeleton

Your face will turn white with fright when you spy this spine-chilling sight!

WHAT YOU'LL NEED

7 white bump chenille stems   Scissors

1 Cut a 2-bump section from a white bump stem. This will be the spine.

2 To make the skull, cut 2 bumps and twist them together so that the thin parts are hidden. Bend the thick parts into a circle, then straighten out the bottom thin parts and twist them together and onto the spine.

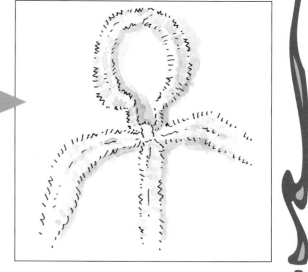

3 Find the middle of a stem and twist it to the spine just under the skull. Bend this stem to form shoulders and arms, cutting the stems to remove most of the thin part of each side and twisting the stem back together to look like elbow joints.

4 Cut a 1-bump piece and twist it to the bottom of the spine. This horizontal piece is the skeleton's hips.

5 Cut another stem in half and twist each piece to 1 side of the hip bone. Bend and twist each leg between bumps to create knees.

6 To make the rib cage, cut four 2-bump pieces and twist them onto the spine. Bend each rib around the spine toward the front of the skeleton.

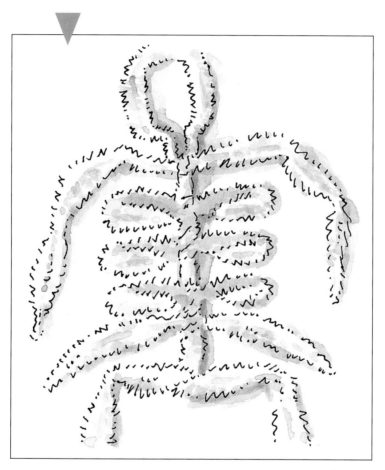

7 Finally, cut the remaining stem into 4 bumps, and bend each bump in half. Twist them to the ends of the arms and legs to create hands and feet.

Halloween Mobile

This Halloween mobile spooks from above. It's more catching than a cobweb in the corner!

WHAT YOU'LL NEED

Tracing paper

Pencil

Scissors

Foam sheet: 5×5 inches yellow; 3×6 inches orange; 3×7 inches white; 5×5 inches black

Paper punch

Fine-point opaque paint markers: brown, black

Thick craft glue

Wiggle eyes: eighteen 12mm; four 5mm

58 inches black satin ribbon, ⅛ inch wide

Ruler

¼-inch black pom

1 Using the patterns on pages 154–155, trace and cut the following shapes from foam: one moon in yellow; two pumpkins in orange; two skulls in white; and one bat, one cat head, and one set of cat paws in black. Use the paper punch to make holes in the foam shapes in the places indicated on the patterns.

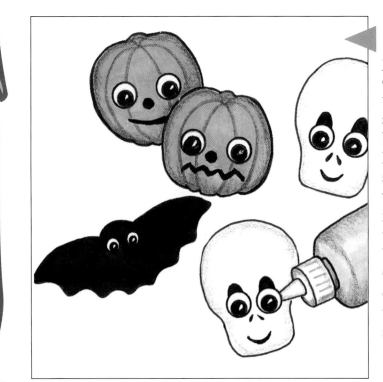

2 Decorate both sides of the pumpkins by drawing lines with the brown marker and faces with the black marker; let dry. Draw faces on both sides of the skulls with the black marker; let dry. Glue two 5mm eyes on both sides of the bat. Glue two 12mm eyes on both sides of the pumpkins and skulls.

3 Cut a 12-inch length of ribbon. Insert one end of the ribbon 1½ inches into the single hole at the top of the moon. Tie a double knot in the ribbon to securely attach it to the moon. Trim the short end of the ribbon close to the knot. Position and glue the cat head on the back upper side of the moon. Position and glue the cat paws on the front of the moon, with the right paw covering the ribbon hanger. Glue the black pom nose on the cat head so that the nose slightly overlaps the edge of the moon, and glue two 12mm eyes to the cat head.

4 Cut the remaining ribbon into the following lengths, and use double knots to tie one end of each length to each foam shape and the other end to a hole at the bottom of the moon: a 6-inch length for one pumpkin; a 9-inch length for one skull; a 13-inch length for the bat; an 11-inch length for one pumpkin; and a 7-inch length for one skull. Trim the ends of each length of ribbon close to the knot.

Trick-or-Treat Bag

Treats taste better when they are tricked out of this boo-tiful bag.

WHAT YOU'LL NEED

Ruler

Brown paper sack (6½×10-inch base, at least 12 inches high)

Pinking shears

Pencil

Tracing paper

Scissors

Shiny paper: 9-inch square white, 9-inch square orange, 2×3 inches yellow, 2-inch square green, 2×3 inches black

Glue stick

Black permanent felt-tipped marker

Glue gun and glue sticks

1½×18 inches white poster board

52-inch length of 1½-inch-wide Halloween print craft ribbon

2 sheets black tissue paper

Have an adult help you when using a glue gun!

1 Use ruler to measure paper sack to 12 inches high. Cut along line with pinking shears.

2 Using patterns on pages 155–156, trace and cut the following: ghost arm, ghost eye crescents, ghost head, and jack-o'-lantern eyes from white shiny paper; jack-o'-lantern top and jack-o'-lantern from orange shiny paper; jack-o'-lantern nose and mouth from yellow shiny paper; jack-o'-lantern stem from green shiny paper; and jack-o'-lantern pupils and ghost eyes from black shiny paper. See page 5 for instructions.

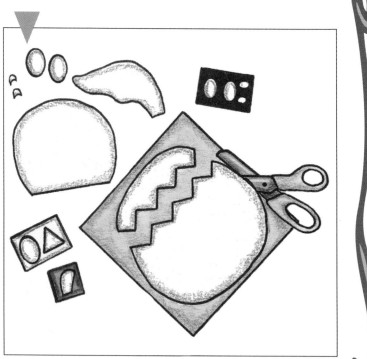

3 Referring to photo, position parts on work surface in the following order: ghost head and arm; jack-o'-lantern top, stem, head, eyes, pupils, nose, and mouth; and ghost eyes and eye crescents. Use glue stick to assemble. Using a black marker, draw eyebrows and mouth on ghost and eyebrows on pumpkin (see finished photograph). Use glue stick to glue entire jack-o'-lantern/ghost piece to the front of the paper sack.

4 To make handle, use a glue gun (set on low) to glue one inch of poster board strip to the top outside middle of the short side of the bag. Repeat on other side of bag with other end of poster board strip. Glue one end of ribbon to bottom middle of bag, across poster board strip, down other side, and across middle of bottom until overlapping other end. Tuck two sheets of black tissue paper inside bag and fill with treats.

Witchy Woman

Create nails that will scare your friends! Bewitching nails are the perfect complement to any costume.

WHAT YOU'LL NEED

Polish remover
Newspaper
Emery board
Hand lotion
Orange wood stick or cuticle pusher

Acrylic paint or nail polish: orange, black, white, yellow
Paintbrush with fine, thin point
Toothpick

Remove all old polish completely. (Be very careful when using polish remover. Always spread a piece of newspaper on your work surface to protect it from any spills.) Using an emery board, shape nails and file away rough edges. Apply a small amount of lotion to each cuticle, and rub it in. Use an orange wood stick or cuticle pusher to push cuticles back. (Never cut cuticles: This can promote infections.) Wash hands well with soap and water.

Spooky Spider Instructions

1 Paint all nails orange. Allow to dry.

2 Using black paint, paint a small circle in the bottom center of each nail.

3 Using black paint and a toothpick, add the spider's legs by painting 4 short lines on each side of the circle.

4 Paint a thin black line from the top of the nail to the spider's body. This is the spider's "web." Allow black paint to dry.

5 Using white paint, paint 2 small crescents on the spider's body for eyes.

Floating Eyes Instructions

1 Paint nails black. Allow to dry.

2 Using white paint, paint 2 pairs of small ovals on the nail. Allow to dry.

3 Using black paint, paint a small dot on each of the white ovals. For fun, place the dots in a different place on each set of eyes so it appears that these "eyeballs" are looking off in different directions.

Candy Corn Instructions

1 Paint nails white. Allow to dry.

4 Using black paint, outline a candy-corn-shape triangle in the center of the nail. Make sure the triangle stretches over all 3 colors.

2 Using orange paint, paint a thick stripe over the middle one-third of the nail. Allow to dry.

5 Using black paint, paint over the entire nail except the center triangle.

3 Using yellow paint, paint the bottom one-third of the nail yellow. Allow to dry.

Rockin' Spider

Your parents might scream when they see this pet, but they won't yell at you to feed it—they'll shriek in horror!

WHAT YOU'LL NEED

Smooth, round rock

Paintbrush

Black acrylic paint

Acrylic gloss medium (optional)

Scissors

2 black chenille stems, at least 12 inches long

Waxed paper or newspaper

Cool-temp glue gun

Glue sticks

Pink dimensional paint (optional)

Tacky glue

2 wiggle eyes

Have an adult help you when using a glue gun!

1 Find a smooth, round rock that fits nicely in the palm of your hand. Wash and dry it.

2 Paint the rock with 2 coats of black acrylic paint. Let paint dry. Then, if you wish, paint on a final coat of shiny acrylic gloss medium.

3 Cut the black chenille stems in half so you have four 6-inch pieces. Shape the ends of each piece to make arched legs. Flatten out the middle of the stems so your rock will fit on top of the stems.

4 Cover your work surface with waxed paper or newspaper. Hold the 4 bent stems together. Apply a generous amount of glue to the flat center area. Put the rock on top of the glue, holding it down until the glue bond sets.

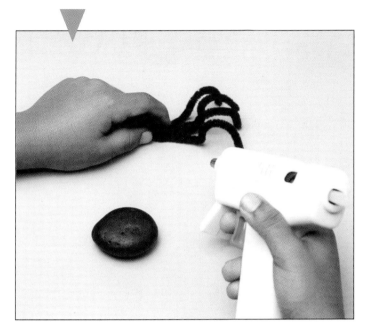

5 If you choose, you may use the pink paint to add a smiling mouth. Using tacky glue, attach the wiggle eyes to the front of your spider.

Spooky Tic-Tac-Toe

Frighten a friend into playing a game of spooky tic-tac-toe. Your friend will fear more than just losing.

WHAT YOU'LL NEED

Magnetic sheeting: one black 5×5-inch piece; one orange and one white 1½×7½-inch piece

Tracing paper

Pencil

Scissors

Manicure scissors

Fine-point opaque paint markers: brown, black

20-inch length of green satin ribbon, ⅛ inch wide

Ruler

Thick craft glue

1 Using the patterns on page 154, trace and cut out five pumpkins from the orange magnetic sheeting and five ghosts from the white magnetic sheeting. When cutting the magnetic sheeting, use regular scissors most of the time, and use manicure scissors for small curves.

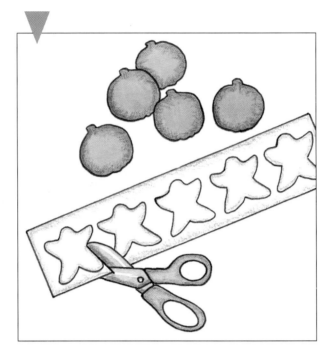

2 Draw the stem and lines on the pumpkins with the brown marker; let dry. Draw faces on the pumpkins with the black marker; let dry.

3 Draw eyes and mouths on the ghosts with the black marker; let dry.

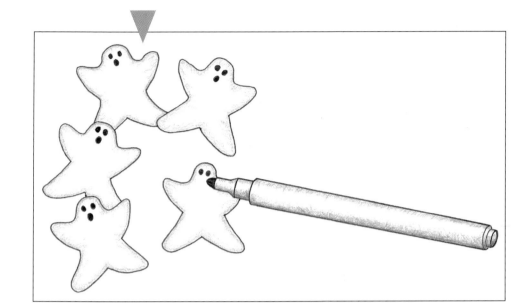

4 Cut the ribbon into four 5-inch lengths. Glue the four lengths of ribbon to the black magnetic sheeting to make a tic-tac-toe grid.

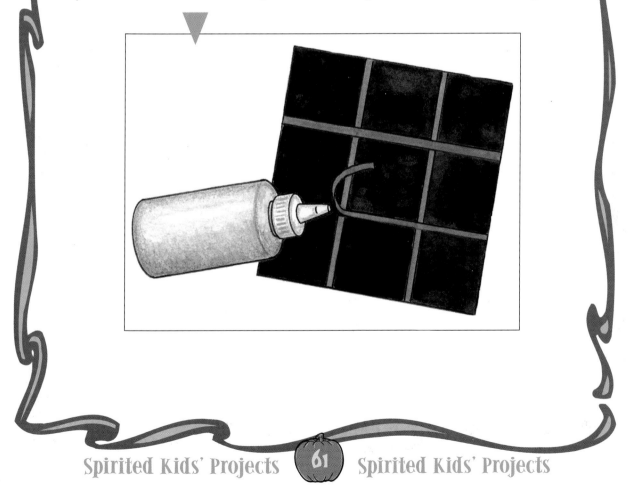

Marvelous Masks

Perfect as quick costumes, these masks won't hide their haunting appeal.

Spider Mask

WHAT YOU'LL NEED

Pencil

Tracing paper

4×8 inches orange poster board

Scissors

Paper punch

Shiny black dimensional paint

Glue stick

2 black poms, 1 inch each

2 black poms, ¾ inch each

Tweezers

4 wiggle eyes, 7mm each

Ruler

Craft snips

2 black chenille stems

Glue gun and glue sticks

22-inch length black yarn; two 4-inch lengths black yarn

14-inch length of ¼-inch-wide white elastic cord

Have an adult help you when using a glue gun!

Spider Mask Instructions

1 Trace mask outline and eye holes onto back of orange poster board according to pattern on page 152. Cut on lines. Punch holes on sides where indicated.

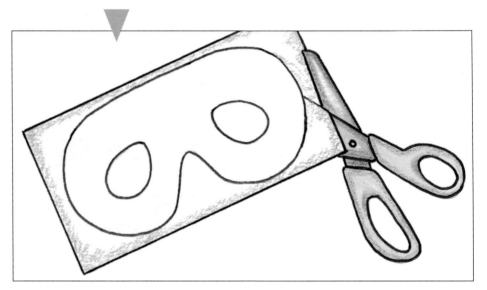

2 Lightly draw pencil web guidelines on front of mask according to spider pattern. Squeeze dimensional paint on web lines; let dry.

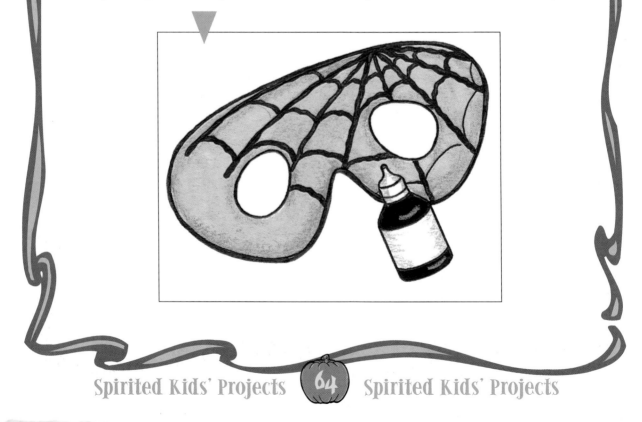

3 Glue together 1-inch and ¾-inch black poms for spider's head and body. Use tweezers to glue two wiggle eyes to front of head. Cut one chenille stem into four 3-inch lengths, using craft snips. Stack and glue middles of four lengths for legs. Glue body to top of leg stack. Bend legs down ½ inch on each end. Bend out ¼ inch on each end for feet. Slightly flatten out legs. Repeat procedure to make another spider but do not flatten legs.

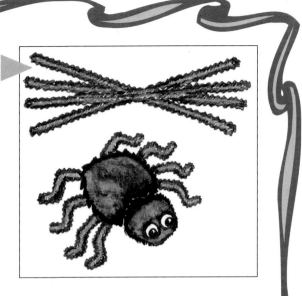

4 Leaving two inches unglued, begin gluing (with glue gun set on low) 22-inch length of yarn about ½ inch above left hole punch, continuing all the way around outside of mask. Glue first spider to top right of mask. Glue dangling end of yarn between second spider's head and body pom. Glue the 4-inch lengths of yarn around eye holes. Paper punch hole on each side of mask as indicated on pattern. Insert ends of 14-inch length elastic cord through holes and tie knots at back of mask—adjust as needed to fit your head. Spot glue elastic knots to hold.

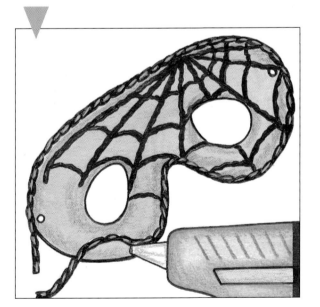

Feather Mask

WHAT YOU'LL NEED

5-inch squares of tissue paper: blue, red, yellow, green

Glue stick

4×8 inches white poster board

Tweezers

Pencil

Tracing paper

Scissors

Paper punch

Glue gun

Glue sticks

Ruler

37-inch length yellow baby rickrack

14-inch length of ¼-inch-wide white elastic cord

6 feathers to match tissue paper, 2 to 4 inches long

Have an adult help you when using a glue gun!

Feather Mask Instructions

1 Rip tissue paper into irregular ½-inch to 1¼-inch pieces. Apply glue stick to poster board. Using tweezers, attach ripped pieces, overlapping edges and randomly placing colors until entire poster board is covered. Turn poster board over. Trace mask outline and eye holes onto poster board using pattern from page 152. Cut on lines. Punch holes on sides where indicated. Turn right side up.

2 Use glue gun (on low) for the following: glue five inches of rickrack, a few inches at a time, around each eye hole. Also, glue 27-inch length of rickrack around outside edge of mask. Attach elastic cord as explained in Step 4 of the spider mask instructions.

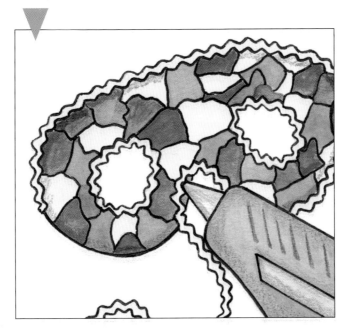

3 Glue ends of three feathers to back top of mask on each side.

Graveyard Grub

Mummy Dogs

1 package (8 breadsticks or 11 ounces) breadstick dough
1 package (16 ounces) hot dogs
Mustard and poppy seeds

◆ Preheat oven to 375°F. Using 1 dough strip for each, wrap hot dogs to look like mummies, leaving opening for eyes. Place on ungreased baking sheet.

◆ Bake 12 to 15 minutes or until light golden brown.

◆ Place dots of mustard and poppy seeds for eyes.   *Makes 8 servings*

Mini Mummy Dogs: Use 1 package (16 ounces) mini hot dogs instead of regular hot dogs. Cut each breadstick strip into 3 pieces. Cut each piece in half lengthwise. Using 1 strip of dough for each, wrap and bake mini hot dogs as directed above.

Mummy Dogs

Grilled Cheese Jack-O'-Lanterns

3 tablespoons butter or margarine, softened
8 slices bread
4 slices Monterey Jack cheese
4 slices sharp Cheddar cheese

◆ Preheat oven to 350°F. Spread butter on one side of each bread slice. Place bread buttered-side-down on ungreased cookie sheet.

◆ Using small sharp hors d'oeuvre cutter or knife, cut out shapes from 4 bread slices to make jack-o'-lantern face. On remaining bread slices layer 1 slice Monterey Jack and 1 slice Cheddar.

◆ Bake 10 to 12 minutes or until cheese is melted. Remove from oven; place jack-o'-lantern bread slice on sandwiches and serve.

Makes 4 servings

Bat & Spook Pizzas

4 (6-inch) Italian bread shells
⅔ cup pizza or spaghetti sauce
1 package (3½ ounces) pepperoni slices
4 slices (1 ounce each) mozzarella cheese

◆ Preheat oven to 375°F. Place bread shells on ungreased baking sheet.

◆ Spread pizza sauce evenly on bread shells; top evenly with pepperoni slices.

◆ Cut out ghost and bat shapes from cheese slices with cookie cutters; place on pizza sauce.

◆ Bake 10 to 12 minutes or until cheese is melted.

Makes 4 servings

Top to bottom: Grilled Cheese Jack-O'-Lanterns and Potato Bugs (page 96)

Eyes of Newt

2 cans (2¼ ounces each) sliced black olives, divided
¼ cup chopped roasted red pepper, divided
1 package (8 ounces) cream cheese, softened
1 clove garlic, minced
8 (6- to 7-inch) flour tortillas
16 slices deli roast beef

◆ Reserve 48 olive slices, 48 pieces red pepper and 1 tablespoon cream cheese.

◆ Chop remaining olives. Combine remaining cream cheese, olives, red pepper and garlic in small bowl; mix well.

◆ Spread about 2 tablespoons cream cheese mixture on each tortilla. Top each tortilla with 2 beef slices, overlapping slightly. Roll up tortillas, jelly-roll fashion. Trim off uneven ends of each tortilla; discard. Slice each tortilla roll into 6 (¾-inch) pieces.

◆ Using reserved cream cheese, attach reserved olives and red pepper to make roll-ups look like eyes.   *Makes 4 dozen pieces*

Sloppy Goblins

1 pound lean ground beef
1 cup chopped onion
4 hot dogs, cut into ½-inch pieces
½ cup ketchup
¼ cup chopped dill pickle
¼ cup honey
¼ cup tomato paste
¼ cup prepared mustard
2 teaspoons cider vinegar
1 teaspoon Worcestershire sauce
8 hamburger buns
Decorations: olives, banana peppers, carrot crinkles, red bell pepper, parsley sprigs and pretzel sticks

◆ Cook beef and onion in large skillet over medium heat until beef is brown and onion is tender; drain. Stir in remaining ingredients except buns and decorations. Cook, covered, 5 minutes or until heated through.

◆ Spoon meat mixture onto bottoms of buns; cover with tops of buns. Serve with decorations and let each person create a goblin face. Refrigerate leftovers.
Makes 8 servings

Top to bottom: Cheesy Bat Biscuits (page 98) and Eyes of Newt

Devilish Delights

1 package (16 ounces) hot roll mix, plus ingredients to prepare mix
1 pound boneless skinless chicken breasts, cut into ¾-inch pieces
2 tablespoons vegetable oil, divided
¾ cup chopped onion
1 clove garlic, minced
1¼ cups sliced zucchini
1 can (8 ounces) peeled diced tomatoes, drained
1 can (4 ounces) sliced mushrooms, drained
1 teaspoon dried basil leaves
½ teaspoon dried oregano leaves
Salt and black pepper
1 cup (4 ounces) shredded mozzarella cheese
1 egg yolk
1 teaspoon water
Red food color

1. Prepare hot roll mix according to package directions. Knead dough on lightly floured surface until smooth, 5 minutes. Cover loosely; let stand 15 minutes.

2. Cook chicken in 1 tablespoon oil in large skillet over medium-high heat 5 to 6 minutes or until no longer pink in center; remove from skillet and set aside. Cook and stir onion and garlic in remaining 1 tablespoon oil in skillet until tender.

3. Stir in zucchini, tomatoes, mushrooms, basil and oregano; bring to a boil. Reduce heat; simmer 5 to 10 minutes or until excess liquid has evaporated. Stir in reserved chicken; cook 1 minute. Remove from heat; season to taste with salt and pepper. Stir in cheese.

4. Preheat oven to 400°F. Grease baking sheets. Roll dough on floured surface to ¼-inch thickness. Cut into equal number of 4-inch circles. Combine scraps and reroll dough if necessary. Place half of circles on prepared baking sheets. Spoon about ¼ cup chicken mixture on half of the circles; top with remaining circles and seal edges with fork. Cut vents to resemble devil; use dough scraps to make horns, eyes, nose and beard.

5. Combine egg yolk and water; brush dough. Add red food color to remaining egg yolk mixture. Brush horns and beard with colored egg mixture.

6. Bake 20 to 25 minutes or until golden. Refrigerate leftovers.
Makes 10 to 12 servings

Top to bottom: Sloppy Goblins (page 72) and Devilish Delight

Halloween Chicken Pizza Masks

1 pound ground chicken
½ cup chopped onion
1 teaspoon salt
1 teaspoon dried oregano
   leaves
½ teaspoon ground black
   pepper
6 English muffins, split
1½ cups prepared pizza
   sauce
1 large green or red bell
   pepper
1 cup (4 ounces)
   shredded Cheddar
   cheese
1 cup (4 ounces)
   shredded mozzarella
   cheese
1 can (2¼ ounces) sliced
   black olives, drained

Heat large skillet over medium-high heat until hot. Add chicken, onion, salt, oregano and black pepper. Cook and stir about 6 minutes or until chicken is no longer pink; set aside. Cover 15½×10½-inch baking pan with foil. Arrange muffins in single layer on prepared pan. Spread 2 tablespoons pizza sauce on each muffin half. Cover generously with chicken mixture, dividing evenly. Cut 12 slivers bell pepper into "smiling" mouth shapes; set aside. Chop remaining bell pepper; sprinkle over mini-pizzas. Combine Cheddar and mozzarella cheeses in small bowl; sprinkle generously over mini-pizzas. Bake at 450°F 12 minutes or until cheese is light brown. Make face on each pizza by using 2 olive slices for "eyes" and 1 pepper shape for "mouth."

Makes 12 mini-pizzas

Favorite recipe from **National Chicken Council**

A bewitching way to garnish a Halloween dish is with vegetable cutouts! Use a small metal cookie cutter or sharp knife to cut Halloween shapes from bell peppers, carrots, parsnips, squash, eggplant or tomatoes.

Halloween Chicken Pizza Masks

Salsa Macaroni & Cheese

1 jar (16 ounces) Ragú®
  Cheese Creations!®
  Double Cheddar
  Sauce
1 cup prepared mild salsa
8 ounces elbow macaroni,
  cooked and drained

1. In 2-quart saucepan, heat Ragú Cheese Creations! Sauce over medium heat. Stir in salsa; heat through.

2. Toss with hot macaroni. Serve immediately.   *Makes 4 servings*

Prep Time: 5 minutes
Cook Time: 15 minutes

Peanut Pitas

1 package (8 ounces)
  small pita breads, cut
  crosswise in half
16 teaspoons reduced-fat
  peanut butter
16 teaspoons strawberry
  spreadable fruit
1 large banana, peeled
  and thinly sliced
  (about 48 slices)

◆ Spread 1 teaspoon each of peanut butter and spreadable fruit inside of each pita half.

◆ Fill pita halves evenly with banana slices. Serve immediately.
    Makes 8 servings

Honey Bees: Substitute honey for spreadable fruit.

Jolly Jellies: Substitute any flavor jelly for spreadable fruit and thin apple slices for banana slices.

Salsa Macaroni & Cheese

Monster Claws

2 tablespoons flour
1 tablespoon plus
    2 teaspoons cajun
    seasoning, divided
1 pound boneless skinless
    chicken breasts, cut
    lengthwise into
    ¾-inch strips
1½ cups cornflake crumbs
2 tablespoons chopped
    green onion
3 eggs, lightly beaten
1 red, yellow or orange
    bell pepper, cut into
    triangle shapes
Barbecue sauce

◆ Preheat oven to 350°F. Lightly grease baking sheet. Place flour and 2 teaspoons cajun seasoning in large resealable food storage bag. Add chicken and seal. Shake bag to coat chicken.

◆ Combine cornflake crumbs, green onion and remaining 1 tablespoon cajun seasoning in large shallow bowl; mix well.

◆ Place eggs in shallow bowl. Dip each chicken strip into eggs and then into crumb mixture. Place coated chicken strips on prepared baking sheets.

◆ Bake chicken strips 8 to 10 minutes or until chicken is no longer pink in center.

◆ When chicken is cool enough to handle, make ½-inch slit in thinner end. Place bell pepper triangle into slit to form claw nail. Serve claws with barbecue sauce for dipping.

Makes about 30 strips

Make dips, sauces or spreads part of the decor too. Serve them in small plastic cauldrons, skulls or jack-o'-lanterns. For a more natural look, serve them in hollowed out miniature pumpkins, or orange or purple bell peppers.

Haunted Taco Tarts

1 tablespoon vegetable oil
½ cup chopped onion
½ pound ground turkey
½ teaspoon chili powder
½ teaspoon dried oregano leaves
1 clove garlic, minced
¼ teaspoon salt
Egg Yolk Paint (recipe follows)
1 package (15 ounces) refrigerated pie crusts
1 egg white
½ cup chopped tomato
½ cup shredded taco-flavored cheese

◆ Heat oil in large skillet over medium heat. Add onion and cook until tender. Add turkey; cook until turkey is no longer pink, stirring occasionally. Stir in seasonings; set aside.

◆ Preheat oven to 375°F. Lightly grease baking sheets. Prepare Egg Yolk Paint; set aside.

◆ On lightly floured surface, roll 1 pie crust to 14-inch diameter. Using 3-inch Halloween cookie cutters, cut out pairs of desired shapes. Repeat with second pie crust, rerolling dough if necessary. Place ½ of shapes on prepared baking sheets. Brush edges with egg white. Spoon about 1 tablespoon taco mixture onto each shape. Sprinkle with 1 teaspoon tomato and 1 teaspoon cheese. Top with remaining matching shapes; press edges to seal. Decorate using Egg Yolk Paint.

◆ Bake 10 to 12 minutes or until golden brown.   *Makes 14 tarts*

Egg Yolk Paint

4 egg yolks, divided
4 teaspoons water, divided
Red, yellow, blue and green liquid food colors

◆ Place 1 egg yolk in each of 4 small bowls. Add 1 teaspoon water and a few drops different food color to each; beat lightly.

Haunted Taco Tarts

Harvest Sticks with Vegetable Dip

2 packages (3 ounces each) cream cheese with chives, softened
1 cup sour cream
⅓ cup finely chopped cucumber
2 tablespoons chopped fresh parsley
2 tablespoons dry minced onion *or* ¼ cup finely chopped fresh onion
1 clove garlic, minced
¼ teaspoon salt
½ teaspoon curry powder (optional)
6 large carrots, peeled
3 medium zucchini

SUPPLIES
Tan raffia

◆ Beat cream cheese in small bowl until fluffy; blend in sour cream. Stir in cucumber, parsley, onion, garlic and salt. Add curry powder, if desired. Spoon into small serving bowl; cover. Refrigerate 1 hour or until serving time.

◆ Just before serving, cut carrots lengthwise into thin strips; gather into bundles. Tie raffia around bundles to hold in place. Repeat with zucchini.

◆ Place bowl of dip on serving tray; garnish, if desired. Surround with bundles of carrots and zucchini.

Makes about 2 cups dip

These vegetable bundles can be made ahead of time. Cut up the vegetables as directed. Place the carrots in a medium bowl; cover with cold water. Refrigerate until ready to use. Place the zucchini sticks in a small resealable plastic food storage bag and refrigerate until ready to use. Just before serving, gather the vegetables into bundles and tie with raffia as directed.

Left to right: Pumpkin Yeast Rolls (page 86) and Harvest Sticks with Vegetable Dip

Pumpkin Yeast Rolls

16 slivered almonds
¼ teaspoon green food color
1 package (16 ounces) hot roll mix
1 to 1¼ teaspoons pumpkin pie spice
⅔ cup apple cider
⅓ cup warm water
2 tablespoons butter, softened
1 whole egg, slightly beaten
1 egg white
2 tablespoons cold water

1. Place almonds in small resealable plastic food storage bag. Add food color; seal bag. Shake bag until almonds are evenly colored. Place almonds on paper-towel-lined plate; let dry.

2. Combine hot roll mix, yeast package from mix and pumpkin pie spice in large bowl; stir to mix well.

3. Combine cider and warm water in small saucepan. Heat over medium heat until cider mixture is hot (120° to 130°F); pour over dry ingredients. Add butter and whole egg; stir until dough pulls away from sides of bowl.

4. Place dough on lightly floured surface; knead until smooth and elastic, about 5 minutes. Let rest 5 minutes. Cut dough into 16 equal pieces; roll each piece into ball. Combine egg white and cold water in small bowl; beat lightly with fork until well blended.

5. Brush egg white mixture evenly onto rolls, covering completely.

6. With sharp knife, lightly score surface of roll, beginning at top center and coming down around sides of rolls, to resemble pumpkin. Insert 1 almond sliver into top of each roll for stem.

7. Lightly grease baking sheet. Place rolls, 2 inches apart, on prepared baking sheet. Cover loosely with towel; let rise in warm place 20 to 30 minutes until doubled in size. Remove towel.

8. Preheat oven to 375°F. Bake 15 to 20 minutes or until golden brown. *Makes 16 rolls*

Individual Mashed Potato Ghosts

5 cups mashed Idaho Potatoes
Waxed paper
½ cup small black olives

1. Cut ghost shapes out of waxed paper.

2. Place templates on serving dish or cookie sheet. Use rubber spatula to mold ½ to 1 cup potatoes into each ghost shape.

3. Slice olives to create circular shapes to be used for eyes and mouth.   *Makes 4 to 6 servings*

Note: To warm Mashed Potato Ghosts, microwave on HIGH 2 to 4 minutes on microwavable plate. If using oven, place potatoes on cookie sheet and re-heat at 350°F, loosely covered with foil, 7 to 8 minutes or until heated through.

*Favorite recipe from **Idaho Potato Commission***

Western Wagon Wheels

1 pound lean ground beef or ground turkey
2 cups wagon wheel pasta, uncooked
1 can (14½ ounces) stewed tomatoes
1½ cups water
1 box (10 ounces) BIRDS EYE® frozen Sweet Corn
½ cup barbecue sauce
Salt and pepper to taste

◆ In large skillet, cook beef over medium heat 5 minutes or until well browned.

◆ Stir in pasta, tomatoes, water, corn and barbecue sauce; bring to a boil.

◆ Reduce heat to low; cover and simmer 15 to 20 minutes or until pasta is tender, stirring occasionally. Season with salt and pepper.   *Makes 4 servings*

Prep Time: 5 minutes
Cook Time: 25 minutes

Serving Suggestion: Serve with corn bread or corn muffins.

Bewitching Bites

Spider Web Dip

Spooky Tortilla Chips (page 90)
1 package (8 ounces) cream cheese, softened
1 jar (8 ounces) prepared salsa
½ cup prepared guacamole
2 tablespoons sour cream

◆ Prepare Spooky Tortilla Chips; set aside.

◆ Place cream cheese and salsa in blender or food processor container; blend until almost smooth.

continued on page 90

Spider Web Dip

Spider Web Dip, continued

◆ Spread cream cheese mixture on round serving dish or pie plate; smooth guacamole over top, leaving ½-inch border. Place sour cream in small resealable plastic food storage bag; seal bag. Cut off tiny corner of bag; pipe sour cream in circles over guacamole. Run tip of knife through sour cream to make "spider web." Serve with Spooky Tortilla Chips.

Makes 8 to 10 servings

Spooky Tortilla Chips

3 packages (12 ounces each) 8-inch plain or flavored flour tortillas
Salt to taste

◆ Preheat oven to 350°F. Spray baking sheet with olive oil nonstick cooking spray.

◆ Using 3-inch Halloween cookie cutters, cut tortillas, one at a time, into shapes. Discard scraps.

◆ Lightly spray tortilla shapes with cooking spray. Place on prepared baking sheet and sprinkle with salt.

◆ Bake 5 to 7 minutes or until edges begin to brown. Remove to wire rack to cool completely.

Makes about 90 chips

Witches' Brew

2 cups apple cider
1½ to 2 cups vanilla ice cream
2 tablespoons honey
½ teaspoon ground cinnamon
¼ teaspoon ground nutmeg

Process cider, ice cream, honey, cinnamon and nutmeg in food processor or blender until smooth. Pour into glasses and sprinkle with additional nutmeg. Serve immediately.

Makes 4 (6-ounce) servings

Prep Time: 10 minutes

Serving Suggestion: Add a few drops of desired food coloring to ingredients in food processor to make a scary brew.

Lighten Up: To reduce fat, replace vanilla ice cream with reduced-fat or fat-free ice cream or frozen yogurt.

Witches' Brew

Creepy Hands

8 cups popped popcorn
1 cup pumpkin seeds, cleaned and patted dry
⅓ cup butter, melted
1 tablespoon Worcestershire sauce
½ teaspoon garlic salt
½ teaspoon seasoned salt
Candy corn

SUPPLIES
6 clear industrial food handler's gloves
Orange and/or black ribbon
6 plastic spider rings

◆ Preheat oven to 300°F. Place popcorn in single layer in 15×10×1-inch jelly-roll pan; sprinkle with pumpkin seeds.

◆ Mix butter, Worcestershire and salts in small bowl. Pour over popcorn; toss to coat.

◆ Bake 30 minutes, stirring after 15 minutes. Cool completely in pan on wire rack.

◆ Place candy corn in end of each glove finger for fingernail; pack glove tightly with popcorn mixture. Close bag tightly at wrist; tie with ribbon. Place ring on 1 finger of each hand.

Makes 6 servings

Monster Eyes

1 container (8 ounces) plain soft cream cheese
6 miniature bagels, split and toasted
6 midget sweet pickles
Red decorating icing

◆ Spread cream cheese evenly onto toasted bagels, leaving center holes in bagels unfrosted.

◆ Cut pickles crosswise in half; insert, cut sides up, into bagel holes. Use icing to add "veins" and "pupils" to eyes as shown.

Makes 12 appetizer servings

Arrange a "boo-tiful" buffet table. Roll up utensils in a festive napkin and use a Halloween cookie cutter as a napkin ring. To keep utensils in easy reach, set them in a black plastic cauldron placed near the plates.

Clockwise from top left: Chocolate Spiders (page 150), Monster Eyes, Doughnut Hole Spider (page 150) and Creepy Hand

Jack-O'-Lantern Cheese Ball

2 cups (8 ounces) shredded Cheddar cheese
4 ounces cream cheese, softened
¼ cup solid-pack pumpkin
¼ cup pineapple preserves
¼ teaspoon ground allspice
¼ teaspoon ground nutmeg
1 pretzel rod, broken in half
Dark rye bread, red pepper and black olive slices
Assorted crackers

◆ Beat cheeses, pumpkin, preserves and spices in medium bowl until smooth. Cover; refrigerate 2 to 3 hours or until cheese is firm enough to shape.

◆ Shape mixture into round pumpkin; place on serving plate. Using knife, score vertical lines down pumpkin. Place pretzel rod in top for stem.

◆ Cut bread into triangles for eyes. Decorate as shown.

◆ Cover loosely; chill until serving time. Serve with crackers.

Makes 16 to 18 servings

Grizzly Gorp

2 cups TEDDY GRAHAM BEARWICH'S® Graham Sandwiches, any flavor
1 cup miniature marshmallows
1 cup dry roasted peanuts
½ cup seedless raisins

In large bowl, combine graham sandwiches, marshmallows, peanuts and raisins. Store in airtight container.

Makes 4½ cups

Haunted Hint

For a traditional costume party, complete with vampires, ghosts and goblins, make a haunted house or coffin invitation. First fold a piece of black paper in half. Cut out a house or coffin shape without cutting completely through the fold. Next cut out a ghost or mummy shape from white paper to fit inside the house or coffin. Write the party information on the ghost or mummy.

Jack-O'-Lantern Cheese Ball

Hot Cocoa with Floating Eyeballs

16 large marshmallows
  Black licorice candies
2 quarts milk
1 cup chocolate-flavored
  drink mix
1 cup mint-flavored
  semisweet chocolate
  chips

SUPPLIES
16 lollipop sticks

◆ Make slit in center of each marshmallow; insert licorice candy into slit. Insert lollipop stick into center of bottom of each eyeball; set aside.

◆ Combine milk and drink mix in medium saucepan. Stir in chocolate chips. Cook over medium heat, stirring occasionally, until chips are melted and milk is heated through.

◆ Place 2 eyeballs in each mug; fill mug with hot cocoa. Serve immediately. *Makes 8 servings*

Potato Bugs

1 package (16 ounces)
  shredded potato
  nuggets
6 pieces uncooked
  spaghetti, broken
  into thirds
1 carrot, cut into 1½-inch
  strips
  Sour cream, black olive
  slices, ketchup and
  broccoli pieces

◆ Preheat oven to 450°F. Lightly grease baking sheets.

◆ Spread potato nuggets on baking sheets. Bake 7 minutes. Loosen nuggets from baking sheets with metal spatula.

◆ Thread 3 potato nuggets onto 1 spaghetti piece. Bake 5 minutes.

◆ Carefully push carrot strips into sides of each nugget for legs. Using sour cream to attach vegetables, decorate faces as shown in photo on page 71.
Makes about 15 servings

Clockwise from top left: Chocolate-Dipped Caramel Apples (page 123), Hot Cocoa with Floating Eyeballs and Tombstone Place Cards (page 131)

Trick or Treats

12 cups popped popcorn
1 pound bacon, fried
    crisp, drained and
    broken into 1-inch
    pieces
1 can (12 ounces) mixed
    nuts, toasted
½ cup sunflower seeds,
    toasted
4 tablespoons butter or
    margarine, melted
    and divided
3 tablespoons grated
    Parmesan cheese,
    divided

Combine popcorn, bacon, nuts and sunflower seeds in large bowl. Drizzle 2 tablespoons butter on mixture. Sprinkle with 4½ teaspoons cheese; toss. Repeat with remaining 2 tablespoons butter and 4½ teaspoons cheese. Serve warm.

Makes 12 (1-cup) servings

Prep Time: 30 minutes

Cook's Note: For a quick and easy way to toast sunflower seeds, use the stove-top method. Spread the seeds in a large dry skillet. Heat over medium-low heat, stirring the seeds or shaking the pan frequently, about 4 to 6 minutes or until the seeds turn golden.

Cheesy Bat Biscuits

1 can (16 ounces) jumbo
    refrigerated
    buttermilk biscuits
3 tablespoons butter,
    melted and divided
¼ cup grated Parmesan
    cheese
1 teaspoon dried parsley
    flakes
1 teaspoon dried basil
    leaves

◆ Preheat oven to 350°F.

◆ Flatten each biscuit into shape until just large enough to fit 3-inch bat cookie cutter. Cut out bat shape; discard scraps. Place biscuits on baking sheet. Lightly score biscuits to outline bat wings; poke holes for eyes with toothpick. Brush biscuits with 1 tablespoon butter. Bake 7 minutes.

◆ Meanwhile, combine cheese, remaining 2 tablespoons butter, parsley and basil in small bowl.

◆ Turn biscuits on end and split into halves with forks. Spread 1 teaspoon cheese mixture on bottom half of each biscuit; replace biscuit top. Bake 3 minutes or until biscuits are golden.   *Makes 8 servings*

Magic Potion

Creepy Crawler Ice Ring

Creepy Crawler Ice Ring (recipe follows)
1 cup boiling water
2 packages (4-serving size each) lime-flavored gelatin
3 cups cold water
1½ quarts carbonated lemon-lime beverage, chilled
½ cup superfine sugar
Gummy worms (optional)

◆ One day ahead, prepare Creepy Crawler Ice Ring.

◆ Pour boiling water over gelatin in heatproof punch bowl; stir until gelatin dissolves. Stir in cold water. Add lemon-lime beverage and sugar; stir well (mixture will foam for several minutes).

◆ Unmold ice ring by dipping bottom of mold briefly into hot water. Float ice ring in punch. Serve cups of punch garnished with gummy worms, if desired.

Makes about 10 servings

1 cup gummy worms or other creepy crawler candy
1 quart lemon-lime thirst quencher beverage

◆ Arrange gummy worms in bottom of 5-cup ring mold; fill mold with thirst quencher beverage. Freeze until solid, 8 hours or overnight.

Haunted Hint

Change this Magic Potion from creepy to cute with just a few simple substitutions. For the punch, use orange-flavored gelatin instead of lime. For the ice ring, use candy corn and candy pumpkins instead of gummy worms.

Eyeballs

12 hard-cooked eggs
1 can (4½ ounces) deviled
  ham
⅓ cup mayonnaise
4 teaspoons prepared
  mustard
¼ cup drained sweet
  pickle relish
12 pimiento-stuffed olives,
  halved

◆ Cut eggs lengthwise into halves. Remove yolks; place in small bowl. Mash egg yolks with fork; mix in deviled ham, mayonnaise, mustard and pickle relish. Season to taste with salt and pepper.

◆ Spoon filling into egg halves. Garnish with olive halves to make "eyeballs."

◆ To make extra-scary bloodshot "eyeballs," spoon ketchup into small resealable plastic food storage bag. Cut off very tiny corner of bag; drizzle over eggs.
Makes 12 servings

Prep Time: 25 minutes

Note: To save time, use leftover ketchup packets to drizzle over eggs to make bloodshot "eyeballs."

Cinnamon Apple Chips

2 cups unsweetened apple
  juice
1 cinnamon stick
2 Washington Red
  Delicious apples

1. In large skillet or saucepan, combine apple juice and cinnamon stick; bring to a low boil while preparing apples.

2. Slice off ½ inch from top and bottom of apples and discard. Stand apples on either cut end; cut crosswise into ⅛-inch-thick slices, rotating apple to cut even slices.

3. Drop slices into boiling juice; cook 4 to 5 minutes or until slices appear translucent and lightly golden. Meanwhile, preheat oven to 250°F.

4. Remove apple slices from juice and pat dry. Arrange slices on wire racks, being sure none overlap. Place racks on middle shelf in oven; bake 30 to 40 minutes until slices are lightly browned and almost dry to touch. Cool completely before storing in airtight container.
Makes about 40 chips

*Favorite recipe from **Washington Apple Commission***

Eyeballs

Trick-or-Treat Punch

Green food color
1 envelope (4 ounces) orange-flavored presweetened drink mix
1 can (12 ounces) frozen lemonade concentrate, thawed
1 bottle (2 liters) ginger ale*

SUPPLIES
1 new plastic household glove

*For an adult party, substitute 2 bottles (750 ml each) champagne for ginger ale, if desired.

◆ One day ahead, fill pitcher with 3 cups water; color with green food color. Pour into glove; tightly secure top of glove with twist tie. Cover baking sheet with paper towels; place glove on prepared baking sheet. Use inverted custard cup to elevate tied end of glove to prevent leaking. Freeze overnight.

◆ When ready to serve, combine drink mix, lemonade concentrate and 4 cups water in large bowl; stir until drink mix is dissolved and mixture is well blended. Pour into punch bowl; add ginger ale.

◆ Cut glove away from ice; float frozen hand in punch.
Makes 16 (6-ounce) servings and 1 ice hand

Make this punch a ghoulish centerpiece. Serve the punch, with the ice hand, in a large plastic black cauldron. Then surround it with an array of spooky treats.

Top to bottom: Trick-or-Treat Punch and Orange Jack-O'-Lanterns (page 142)

Tricky Treats

Ghost on a Stick

4 medium pears, stems removed
9 squares (2 ounces each) almond bark
  Mini chocolate chips

SUPPLIES
  4 wooden craft sticks

◆ Line baking sheet with waxed paper. Insert sticks into stem ends of pears. Melt bark according to package directions. Dip pear into bark, spooning over top to coat evenly. Remove excess by scraping pear bottom across rim of measuring cup. Place on baking cup; let set 1 minute. Decorate with chocolate chips. Repeat with remaining pears. Place spoonful of extra almond bark at bottom of pears for ghost tails. Refrigerate until firm.   *Makes 4 servings*

Left to right: Monster Munch (page 113) and Ghost on a Stick

Little Devils

1 package (1 pound
  2 ounces) carrot
  cake mix
½ cup solid-pack pumpkin
⅓ cup vegetable oil
3 eggs
1 container (16 ounces)
  cream cheese frosting
Assorted Halloween
  candies, jelly beans,
  chocolate candies and
  nuts

◆ Preheat oven to 350°F. Prepare cake mix according to package directions, using water as directed on package, pumpkin, oil and eggs. Spoon batter into 18 paper-lined muffin cups. Bake 20 minutes or until toothpick inserted in centers of cupcakes comes out clean. Cool in pans on wire rack 5 minutes; remove and cool completely.

◆ Frost cupcakes with frosting; let goblin guests decorate their own with assorted candies.

Makes 18 cupcakes

Make-Ahead Time: up to 3 days in refrigerator or up to 1 month in freezer before serving

Final Prep Time: 20 minutes

Spiders

1 (3-inch) oatmeal cookie
1 tablespoon Fluffy White
  Frosting (page 128)
1 small black jelly bean
1 large black jelly bean
1 black licorice whip
2 red candy-coated
  licorice pieces

Frost oatmeal cookie with Fluffy White Frosting. Arrange jelly beans on cookies to make spider head and body. Cut 6 to 8 licorice whip pieces (about 1½ inches long); curve and position for legs. Add red candy antennae to head.

Makes 1 cookie

If weather permits, a treasure hunt in the backyard is a great party activity. Some fun prizes to hide are decorated pencils and erasers, stickers, pennies, wrapped candies and small toys, such as spider rings.

Little Devils

Full-Moon Pumpkin Cheesecake

**Gingersnap Cookie
Crust (page 112)**
**4 packages (8 ounces
each) cream cheese,
softened**
½ cup sugar
6 eggs
1 cup sour cream
1 cup solid pack pumpkin
**2 tablespoons all-purpose
flour**
**2 teaspoons ground
cinnamon**
½ teaspoon ground ginger
**½ teaspoon ground
allspice**
**3 ounces semisweet
chocolate, melted**
**1 recipe Black Cat Fudge
(page 112)**

◆ Prepare Gingersnap Cookie
Crust; set aside.

◆ *Increase oven temperature to
425°F.* Beat cream cheese in
large bowl until fluffy; beat in
sugar and eggs, one at a time. Add
sour cream, pumpkin, flour and
spices; beat well. Pour 2 cups
batter into small bowl; stir in
chocolate.

◆ Pour remaining batter into
prepared crust. Spoon chocolate
batter in large swirls over batter
in pan; draw knife through
mixture to marbleize.

◆ Bake 15 minutes. *Reduce oven
temperature to 300°F.* Bake
45 minutes (center of
cheesecake will not be set). Turn
oven off; let cheesecake stand in
oven with door slightly ajar
1 hour. Cool to room temperature
in pan on wire rack. Cover;
refrigerate in pan overnight.

◆ Prepare Black Cat Fudge; do
not cut. Using diagram below as
guide, cut out witch shape. Score
with knife. Cut small star shapes
from scraps with cutter.

◆ Remove side of pan from
cheesecake; place cheesecake on
serving plate. Carefully position
witch on cheesecake as shown
in photo. Position stars as shown.
Makes about 15 servings

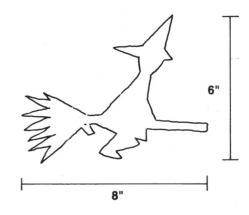

continued on page 112

Full-Moon Pumpkin Cheesecake

Full-Moon Pumpkin Cheesecake, continued

Gingersnap Cookie Crust

1 cup gingersnap cookie crumbs
½ cup chopped pecans
¼ cup butter or margarine, melted

◆ Preheat oven to 350°F. Combine cookie crumbs and nuts in small bowl. Mix in butter.

◆ Press mixture on bottom and 1-inch up side of 9-inch springform pan.

◆ Bake 8 minutes; cool.

Black Cat Fudge

8 ounces semisweet chocolate, coarsely chopped
¼ cup butter or margarine
⅓ cup light corn syrup
¼ cup whipping cream
1 teaspoon vanilla
¼ teaspoon salt
4½ cups powdered sugar, sifted
30 vanilla milk chips

◆ Line 11×7-inch pan with foil, extending foil beyond edges of pan; grease foil.

◆ Melt chocolate and butter in medium saucepan over low heat; stir in corn syrup, cream, vanilla and salt. Remove from heat; stir in sugar until smooth. Spread in prepared pan. Chill until firm, 1 to 2 hours.

◆ Remove fudge from pan using foil; peel off foil. Following diagram, cut out cats. Clean knife often to prevent sticking. Place 2 vanilla chips on each for eyes. Score feet for claws. Cover and chill.   *Makes about 1½ pounds (12 to 15 cats)*

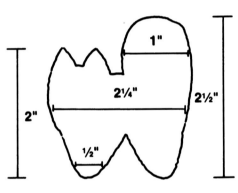

Monster Munch

**6 squares (2 ounces each)
    almond bark, divided
1½ cups pretzel sticks
    Orange food coloring
2 cups graham cereal
¾ cup Halloween colored
    candy-coated
    chocolate pieces
¾ cup miniature
    marshmallows
½ cup chocolate sprinkles**

◆ Place 1½ squares almond bark in small microwavable bowl. Microwave at MEDIUM (50% power) 1 minute; stir. Repeat steps as necessary, stirring at 15-second intervals, until completely melted.

◆ Place pretzel sticks in large bowl. Add melted almond bark and stir until all pieces are coated. Spread coated pretzel sticks out on waxed paper, separating pieces; let set.

◆ Place remaining 4½ squares almond bark in medium microwavable bowl. Microwave at MEDIUM (50% power) 1 minute; stir. Repeat steps as necessary, stirring at 15-second intervals, until completely melted. Stir in food coloring until almond bark is bright orange.

◆ Place cereal in large bowl. Add half of orange-colored almond bark and stir until cereal is evenly coated. Add chocolate pieces, marshmallows and remaining almond bark; stir until mix is evenly coated. Stir in pretzel sticks.

◆ Break mix into small clusters and spread out on waxed paper. Immediately sprinkle clusters with chocolate sprinkles; let set.
Makes about 5 cups snack mix

Serve this sweet snack mix in a home-made candy corn bowl! Start with any size clean terra cotta flower pot. Paint the bottom white, the middle orange and the top yellow. To use for serving, plug the bottom hole with aluminum foil and fill with candy, nuts or snack mix.

Boo the Ghost

1 (13×9-inch) cake,
   completely cooled
2 cups Light & Fluffy
   Frosting (recipe
   follows)
2 black licorice drops or
   jelly beans

SUPPLIES
1 (19×13) cake board, cut
   in half crosswise and
   covered
Plastic spiders
   (optional)

Light & Fluffy Frosting

⅔ cups sugar
2 egg whites*
5 teaspoons light corn
   syrup
Dash salt
1 teaspoon vanilla

*Use only Grade A clean, uncracked eggs.

Combine sugar, egg whites, corn syrup and salt in top of double boiler. Set over boiling water. Beat constantly until stiff peaks form, about 7 minutes. Remove from heat; beat in vanilla.

◆ If cake top is rounded, trim horizontally with long serrated knife. Trim sides of cake.

◆ Using photo as guide, draw ghost outline on 13×9-inch piece of waxed paper. Cut pattern out and place on cake. Cut out ghost. Place on prepared cake board.

◆ Prepare Light & Fluffy Frosting. Frost ghost, swirling frosting. Arrange licorice drops for eyes and spiders as shown in photo.

Makes 12 to 14 servings

Haunted Hint

Cake boards are made of sturdy cardboard and are available in various sizes and shapes in craft and kitchenware stores. They can be covered with foil, paper doilies or plastic wrap. If a cake is very heavy, stack two cake boards together before covering for additional support.

Boo the Ghost

Black Cat Cookies

1 package refrigerated
  sugar cookie dough
White Decorator Icing
  (recipe follows)
Black food coloring
Assorted candies

◆ Preheat oven to 350°F. Remove dough from wrapper according to package directions. Divide dough into 2 equal sections. Reserve 1 section; cover and refrigerate remaining section.

◆ Roll reserved dough on lightly floured surface to ⅛-inch thickness. Sprinkle with flour to minimize sticking, if necessary.

◆ Cut out cookies using 3½-inch cat face cookie cutter. Place 2 inches apart on ungreased baking sheets. Repeat with remaining dough and scraps.

◆ Bake 8 to 10 minutes or until firm but not browned. Cool on baking sheets 2 minutes. Remove to wire rack; cool completely.

◆ Prepare White Decorator Icing. Add desired amount of food coloring to make black. Decorate cookies with icing and candies as shown in photo.

Makes about 20 cookies

White Decorator Icing

4 cups powdered sugar
½ cup vegetable
  shortening or
  unsalted butter
1 tablespoon corn syrup
6 to 8 tablespoons milk

◆ Beat sugar, shortening, corn syrup and milk in medium bowl 2 minutes or until fluffy.

Give your guests goosebumps when you present "A Ghost's Tale." Turn off all the lights and then read a spine-tingling story by candlelight or flashlight. Have another adult or older child behind the party guests, making eerie sound effects to go with the story.

Black Cat Cookies

Candy Corn Cookies

Butter Cookie dough (recipe follows)
Cookie Glaze (recipe follows)
Yellow and orange food colors

◆ Preheat oven to 350°F.

◆ Roll dough on floured surface to ¼-inch thickness. Using photo as guide, cut out 3-inch candy corn shapes. Place cutouts on ungreased cookie sheets.

◆ Bake 8 to 10 minutes or until edges are lightly browned. Remove to wire racks to cool completely. Prepare Cookie Glaze.

◆ Place racks over waxed-paper-covered baking sheets. Divide Cookie Glaze into thirds; place in separate small bowls. Color ⅓ of glaze with yellow food color and ⅓ with orange food color. Leave remaining glaze white. Spoon different colored glazes over cookies to resemble "candy corn" as shown in photo. Let stand until glaze is set.

Makes about 2 dozen cookies

Butter Cookie Dough

[handwritten: 2c.] ¾ cup butter, softened
[handwritten: ½ c.] ¼ cup granulated sugar
[handwritten: ½ c.] ¼ cup packed light brown sugar
[handwritten: 2] 1 egg yolk
[handwritten: 4c.] 1¾ cups all-purpose flour
[handwritten: 2 tsp] ¾ teaspoon baking powder
[handwritten: 1 tsp] ⅛ teaspoon salt

[handwritten: 2 tsp vanilla]

◆ Combine butter, granulated sugar, brown sugar and egg yolk in medium bowl. Add flour, baking powder and salt; mix well.

◆ Cover; refrigerate about 4 hours or until firm.

Cookie Glaze: Combine 4 cups powdered sugar and 4 tablespoons milk in small bowl. Add 1 to 2 tablespoons more milk as needed to make medium-thick, pourable glaze.

Bat Cookies: Omit yellow and orange food colors. Prepare recipe as directed except use bat cookie cutter to cut out cookies. Bake as directed. Color glaze with black paste food color; spoon over cookies. Decorate with assorted candies as shown in photo.

Top to bottom: Bat Cookies and Candy Corn Cookies

Scarecrow Cupcakes

1¼ cups all-purpose flour
¾ teaspoon baking
    powder
½ teaspoon baking soda
¼ teaspoon salt
¾ teaspoon ground
    cinnamon
⅛ teaspoon ground cloves
⅛ teaspoon ground
    nutmeg
⅛ teaspoon ground
    allspice
¾ cup heavy cream
2 tablespoons molasses
¼ cup butter, softened
¼ cup sugar
¼ cup packed brown
    sugar
2 eggs
½ teaspoon vanilla extract
¾ cup sweetened
    shredded coconut
Maple Buttercream
    Frosting (page 122)
Toasted coconut, chow
    mein noodles,
    shredded wheat
    cereal, candy corn,
    candy-coated
    chocolate pieces,
    gumdrops and
    decorator gel

◆ Preheat oven to 350°F. Line 18 (2¾-inch) muffin cups with paper baking liners. Mix flour, baking powder, baking soda, salt and spices in medium bowl; set aside. Mix cream and molasses in small bowl; set aside.

◆ Beat butter in large bowl until creamy. Add sugars; beat until light and fluffy. Add eggs, one at a time, beating well after each addition. Blend in vanilla.

◆ Add flour mixture alternately with cream mixture, beating well after each addition. Stir in coconut; spoon batter into prepared muffin cups, filling about half full.

◆ Bake 20 to 25 minutes or until wooden toothpick inserted in centers comes out clean. Cool in pan on wire rack 10 minutes. Remove cupcakes to racks; cool.

◆ Prepare Maple Buttercream Frosting. Frost cupcakes and decorate to make scarecrow faces as shown in photo.

Makes 18 servings
continued on page 122

Scarecrow Cupcakes, continued

Maple Buttercream Frosting

2 tablespoons butter, softened
2 tablespoons maple or pancake syrup
1½ cups powdered sugar

◆ Beat butter and syrup in medium bowl until blended. Gradually beat in powdered sugar until smooth.

Makes about 1½ cups

To make a gumdrop hat, roll out a large gumdrop on a generously sugared surface. Cut 1 rounded piece to look like the top of the hat and 1 straight piece to look like the brim of the hat as shown in the photo. Overlap the pieces to make the hat; pipe decorator gel over the seam for the hat band.

Boo Bites

¼ cup (½ stick) butter or margarine
30 large marshmallows *or* 3 cups miniature marshmallows
¼ cup light corn syrup
½ cup REESE'S® Creamy Peanut Butter
⅓ cup HERSHEY'S Semi-Sweet Chocolate Chips
4½ cups crisp rice cereal

Line cookie sheet with wax paper.

Melt butter in large saucepan over low heat. Add marshmallows. Cook, stirring constantly, until marshmallows are melted. Remove from heat. Add corn syrup; stir until well blended. Add peanut butter and chocolate chips; stir until chips are melted and mixture is well blended.

Add cereal; stir until evenly coated. Cool slightly. With wet hands, shape mixture into 1½-inch balls; place balls on prepared cookie sheet. Cool completely. Store in tightly covered container in cool, dry place.

Makes about 4 dozen pieces

Chocolate-Dipped Caramel Apples

1 package (14 ounces) caramels
1 tablespoon water
6 medium apples
4 ounces milk or semisweet chocolate confectionary coating, coarsely chopped
White decorating icing
Candy corn, gummy worms and assorted candies

SUPPLIES
6 wooden craft sticks

◆ Cover baking sheet with waxed paper. Unwrap caramels. Combine caramels and water in medium saucepan; cook over medium heat, stirring constantly, until caramels are melted.

◆ Rinse and thoroughly dry apples; insert wooden sticks into stem ends. Dip apples, 1 at a time, into caramel mixture, coating completely. Remove excess caramel mixture by scraping apple bottom across rim of saucepan. Place on waxed paper.

◆ Place confectionary coating in small saucepan. Cook over low heat, stirring frequently, until chocolate is melted. Dip apples halfway into chocolate. Return to waxed paper.

◆ Use icing to write names on apples. Use small amount of additional icing to secure desired decorations on apples. Chill until firm. *Makes 6 servings*

Not only can these apples guide your guests to their seats, they make a yummy take-home treat! Simply wrap them up in plastic wrap and tie with black and orange ribbons.

Jack-O'-Lantern

2 (10-inch) Bundt cakes
2 recipes Buttercream
    Frosting (recipe
    follows)
Orange, green and
    brown paste food
    colors
Candy corn

SUPPLIES
2 (10-inch) round cake
    boards, stacked and
    covered, or large
    plate
1 (6-ounce) paper cup or
    ice cream wafer cone
Pastry bag and medium
    writing tip

◆ Prepare 2 recipes Buttercream Frosting. Tint 4½ cups frosting orange, ½ cup dark green and ¼ cup dark brown. To tint frosting, add small amount of desired paste color with toothpick; stir well. Slowly add more color until frosting is desired shade.

◆ Trim flat sides of cakes. Place one cake on prepared cake board, flat-side up. Frost top of cake with some of the orange frosting. Place second cake, flat side down, over frosting.

◆ Frost entire cake with orange frosting.

◆ Hold cup over fingers of one hand. Using other hand, frost cup with green frosting. Place upside-down in center of cake to form stem. Touch up frosting, if needed.

◆ Using writing tip and brown frosting, pipe eyes and mouth. Arrange candy corn for teeth as shown in photo. Before serving, remove stem. Slice and serve top cake first, then bottom.

Makes 36 to 40 servings

Buttercream Frosting

6 cups powdered sugar,
    sifted and divided
¾ cup butter, softened
¼ cup shortening
6 to 8 tablespoons milk,
    divided
1 teaspoon vanilla

◆ Combine 3 cups powdered sugar, butter, shortening, 4 tablespoons milk and vanilla in large bowl. Beat with electric mixer until smooth. Add remaining powdered sugar; beat until light and fluffy, adding more milk, 1 tablespoon at a time, as needed for good spreading consistency.

Makes about 3½ cups

Jack-O'-Lantern

Chocolate Spider Web Cake

1⅔ cups all-purpose flour
1½ cups sugar
 ½ cup HERSHEY'S Cocoa
1½ teaspoons baking soda
 1 teaspoon salt
 ½ teaspoon baking
    powder
 2 eggs
1½ cups buttermilk or sour
    milk*
 ½ cup shortening (do not
    use butter, margarine,
    spread or oil)
 1 teaspoon vanilla extract
   One-Bowl Buttercream
    Frosting (recipe
    follows)
   Spider Web (page 128)

*To sour milk: Use 4½ teaspoons white vinegar plus milk to equal 1½ cups.

1. Heat oven to 350°F. Thoroughly grease and flour two 9-inch round baking pans.

2. Combine dry ingredients in large bowl; add eggs, buttermilk, shortening and vanilla. Beat on low speed of mixer 1 minute, scraping bowl constantly. Beat on high speed 3 minutes, scraping bowl occasionally. Pour batter into prepared pans.

3. Bake 30 to 35 minutes or until wooden pick inserted in center comes out clean. Cool 10 minutes; remove from pans to wire racks. Cool completely.

4. Frost with One-Bowl Buttercream Frosting. Immediately pipe or drizzle Spider Web in 4 or 5 circles on top of cake. Using a knife or wooden pick, immediately draw 8 to 10 lines from center to edges of cake at regular intervals to form web. Garnish with a "spider," using a cookie, licorice and other candies.

Makes 12 servings

One-Bowl Buttercream Frosting

6 tablespoons butter or
    margarine, softened
2⅔ cups powdered sugar
 ½ cup HERSHEY'S Cocoa
 4 to 6 tablespoons milk
 1 teaspoon vanilla extract

Beat butter; add powdered sugar and cocoa alternately with milk, beating to spreading consistency. Stir in vanilla.

Makes about 2 cups frosting.
continued on page 128

Chocolate Spider Web Cake

Chocolate Spider Web Cake, continued

Spider Web: Place ½ cup HERSHEY'S Premier White Chips and ½ teaspoon shortening (do not use butter, margarine, spread or oil) in small heavy seal-top plastic bag. Microwave at HIGH (100%) 45 seconds. Squeeze gently. If necessary, microwave an additional 10 to 15 seconds; squeeze until chips are melted. With scissors, make small diagonal cut in bottom corner of bag; squeeze mixture onto cake as directed.

If your party is in the backyard or in the basement, have guests enter at the front door of the house and go through a maze of furniture, cardboard or sheets to get to the entrance of the party. Make the maze creepy with dim lights, terrifying sounds and plenty of cobwebs!

Funny Bug

1 (3-inch) oatmeal cookie
1 tablespoon Fluffy White Frosting (recipe follows)
2 miniature chocolate sandwich cookies
1 red gumdrop
2 cheese corn curls

Frost oatmeal cookie with Fluffy White Frosting. Arrange sandwich cookies to make eyes. Attach gumdrop mouth and corn curl antennae.   *Makes 1 cookie*

Fluffy White Frosting: Mix 1 (16-ounce) container vanilla frosting and ¾ cup marshmallow creme in medium bowl; mix well. Makes about 2 cups.

Clockwise from top left: Funny Bugs, Spider (page 108), Spooky Ghost Cookies (page 130), Bloodshot Eyeballs (page 134)

Spooky Ghost Cookies

1 recipe Butter Cookie
  Dough (page 118)
1 recipe Fluffy White
  Frosting (page 128)
½ cup semisweet
  chocolate chips
  (about 60 chips)

◆ Preheat oven to 350°F. Roll dough on floured surface to ¼-inch thickness. Cut out ghost shapes using 3-inch cookie cutter.

◆ Bake on ungreased cookie sheets 10 to 12 minutes until edges begin to brown. Remove to wire racks; cool completely.

◆ Prepare Fluffy White Frosting. Spread frosting over cookies, swirling to give ghostly appearance. Position 2 chocolate chips on each cookie for eyes.

Makes about 2½ dozen cookies

Magic Dip

1 package (8 ounces)
  PHILADELPHIA®
  Cream Cheese,
  softened
1 cup BAKER'S® Semi-
  Sweet Real Chocolate
  Chips
½ cup BAKER'S® ANGEL
  FLAKE® Coconut,
  toasted
½ cup chopped peanuts
  Graham crackers

SPREAD cream cheese on bottom of 9-inch microwavable pie plate or quiche dish.

TOP with remaining ingredients.

MICROWAVE on MEDIUM (50% power) 3 to 4 minutes or until warm. Serve with graham crackers. Garnish, if desired.

Makes 6 to 8 servings

Prep Time: 5 minutes
Microwave Time: 4 minutes

Tombstone Place Cards

½ container (16 ounces) vanilla frosting
8 (2×1¼-inch) fudge-coated graham cracker cookies
8 fun-size (2-inch) milk-chocolate-covered caramel candy bars
½ container (16 ounces) chocolate frosting
4 whole graham crackers
Pumpkin candies
½ cup sweetened shredded coconut, tinted green

SUPPLIES
Pastry bag and small writing tip

◆ Spoon vanilla frosting into pastry bag fitted with writing tip; use to write names on fudge-coated graham cracker cookies.

◆ Cover tops of candy bars with small amount of chocolate frosting; stand fudge-coated graham crackers upright on candy bars to form tombstone shapes.

◆ Break graham crackers in half crosswise; spread tops with chocolate frosting. Position candy tombstones and pumpkins in chocolate frosting on graham crackers; sprinkle with coconut to resemble grass.

Makes 8 place cards

To tint coconut green, add a few drops of green food color and ¼ teaspoon water to a large resealable plastic food storage bag. Add ½ cup sweetened shredded coconut. Seal the bag and shake it until the coconut is evenly colored.

Ghoulish Delights

Skull & Cross Bones

1 package (21.5 ounces) brownie mix, plus ingredients to
   prepare mix
1 egg white
⅛ teaspoon almond extract, optional
¼ cup sugar
   Red and black decorator gels
1 container (16 ounces) prepared chocolate frosting

SUPPLIES
   Pastry bag with medium writing tip

◆ Prepare and bake brownies in 13×9-inch baking pan according to
package directions. Cool completely.

◆ Preheat oven to 250°F. Line baking sheet with parchment paper.

continued on page 134

Skull & Cross Bones, continued

◆ Beat egg white in large bowl until foamy. Add almond extract, if desired; beat until soft peaks form. Gradually add sugar; beat until stiff peaks form.

◆ Fill pastry bag with egg white mixture. Pipe 24 skull and cross bones shapes onto prepared baking sheet. Bake about 12 minutes or until set. Cool on pan on wire racks. Carefully remove meringues from parchment paper. Decorate with red gel for eyes and black gel for mouths.

◆ Frost brownies and cut into 24 rectangles. Place one meringue on each brownie.

Makes 2 dozen brownies

Get everyone involved in your Halloween party! Have adults or older kids dress up in scary costumes and be camouflaged in the haunted setting. They can pop out at a prearranged time for maximum frightfulness.

Bloodshot Eyeballs

2 fudge-covered chocolate sandwich cookies
1 tablespoon Fluffy White Frosting (recipe follows)
2 green jelly beans
Red decorating gel

Frost cookies with Fluffy White Frosting, leaving edge of cookie showing. Press jelly beans into frosting to make pupils of eyes. Decorate with red gel to make eyes look bloodshot.

Makes 2 eyeballs

Fluffy White Frosting: Mix 1 (16-ounce) container vanilla frosting and ¾ cup marshmallow creme in medium bowl; mix well. Makes about 2 cups.

The Big Spider Web

1½ cups all-purpose flour
½ teaspoon baking soda
¾ cup creamy peanut
    butter
½ cup margarine or
    butter, softened
1¼ cups firmly packed light
    brown sugar
2 teaspoons vanilla
    extract
1 egg
¾ cup milk chocolate
    chips, divided
½ cup PLANTERS® Dry
    Roasted Peanuts,
    chopped
1 cup marshmallow fluff
Assorted candies and
    gummy creatures

Combine flour and baking soda; set aside.

In large bowl, with electric mixer at medium speed, beat peanut butter, margarine, sugar and vanilla until creamy. Beat in egg until light and fluffy; gradually blend in flour mixture. Stir in ½ cup chocolate chips and chopped peanuts.

Press dough into greased 14-inch pizza pan. Bake at 350°F for 20 to 25 minutes or until done. Cool completely in pan on wire rack. Frost top of cookie with marshmallow fluff to within 1 inch of edge. Melt remaining ¼ cup chocolate chips; drizzle chocolate in circular pattern over marshmallow. Draw knife through marshmallow topping to create web effect. Decorate with assorted candies and gummy creatures.   *Makes 16 servings*

Haunted Hint

Halloween is the perfect time to have a theme party! Choose a theme that has a wide variety of costume options, such as "A Trip to the Zoo," "Under the Sea" or "The Insect World." Make the invitations, food, decorations, and even the games reflect the theme.

Witch Cake

1 package (2-layer size) cake mix, any flavor, plus ingredients to prepare mix
2 containers (16 ounces each) vanilla frosting
Green paste food color
Black decorating gel
Black paste food color
Red licorice whips
1 sugar cone
Assorted candies
Red chewy fruit snack roll-up cutouts

SUPPLIES
1 (15×10-inch) cake board, covered, or large tray
Pastry bag and medium star tip
1 purchased witch's black hat

◆ Preheat oven to 350°F. Grease and flour 13×9-inch baking pan.

◆ Prepare cake according to package directions; pour batter into prepared pan.

◆ Bake 30 to 35 minutes or until wooden toothpick inserted into center comes out clean. Cool in pan on wire rack 10 minutes. Remove from pan to rack; cool.

◆ If cake top is rounded, trim horizontally with long serrated knife. Place cake on prepared cake board. Spread top and sides of cake with 1 container frosting. Transfer about half of remaining container frosting to small bowl; color with green food color.

◆ Using photo as guide, trace outline of witch's head onto frosted cake with toothpick. Fill in face with thin layer of green frosting; outline with decorating gel as shown in photo.

◆ Place remaining frosting in another small bowl; color with black paste food color. Spoon into pastry bag fitted with star tip; pipe frosting around edges of cake.

◆ Cut hat in half lengthwise. Place one half on cake; discard remaining half. Cut licorice into desired lengths. Place around hat to resemble hair as shown in photo.

◆ Place sugar cone on cake for nose. Use candies and fruit snack cutouts to make eyes and mouth.

Makes 12 servings

Coffin Cookies

1 package (18 ounces)
  refrigerated chocolate
  cookie dough*
Marshmallow Filling
  (recipe follows)
Colored sprinkles,
  sugars and decors
White decorating icing

*If refrigerated chocolate cookie dough is unavailable, add ¼ cup unsweetened cocoa powder to refrigerated sugar cookie dough. Beat in large bowl until well blended.

◆ Draw pattern for coffin on cardboard following diagram; cut out pattern.

◆ Preheat oven to 350°F. Remove dough from wrapper according to package directions. Divide dough into 2 equal sections. Reserve 1 section; cover and refrigerate remaining section.

◆ Roll reserved dough on lightly floured surface to ⅛-inch thickness. Sprinkle with flour to minimize sticking, if necessary.

◆ Place pattern on cookie dough; cut dough around pattern with sharp knife. Repeat as necessary. Place cookies 2 inches apart on ungreased baking sheets. Repeat with remaining dough and scraps.

◆ Bake about 6 minutes or until firm but not browned. Cool on baking sheets 2 minutes. Remove to wire rack; cool completely.

◆ Prepare Marshmallow Filling. Spread half of cookies with 2 teaspoons filling each; top with remaining cookies. Roll cookie sandwich edges in sprinkles.

◆ Decorate as desired.

Makes about 2 dozen sandwich cookies

Marshmallow Filling

1 cup prepared vanilla
  frosting
¾ cup marshmallow
  creme

◆ Combine frosting and marshmallow creme in small bowl until well blended.

¾"

1"

2½"

½"

Coffin Cookies

Graveyard Treat

2¼ cups chocolate wafer cookie crumbs, divided

½ cup sugar, divided

½ cup (1 stick) margarine or butter, melted

1 package (8 ounces) PHILADELPHIA® Cream Cheese, cubed, softened

1 tub (12 ounces) COOL WHIP® Whipped Topping, thawed

2 cups boiling water

1 package (8-serving size) or 2 packages (4-serving size) JELL-O® Brand Orange Flavor Gelatin

½ cup cold water

    Ice cubes

    Rectangular or oval-shaped sandwich cookies

    Decorator icings

    Candy corn and pumpkins

BEAT cream cheese and remaining ¼ cup sugar in medium bowl with wire whisk until smooth. Gently stir in ½ of the whipped topping. Spread evenly over crust.

STIR boiling water into gelatin in medium bowl 2 minutes or until completely dissolved. Mix cold water and ice cubes to make 1½ cups. Add to gelatin; stir until slightly thickened (consistency of unbeaten egg whites). Remove any remaining ice. Spoon gelatin over cream cheese layer.

REFRIGERATE 3 hours or until firm. Spread remaining whipped topping over gelatin just before serving; sprinkle with remaining ¼ cup cookie crumbs. Decorate sandwich cookies with icings to make "tombstones." Stand tombstones on top of dessert with candies to resemble a graveyard. Cut into squares to serve. *Makes 15 to 18 servings*

MIX 2 cups of the cookie crumbs, ¼ cup of the sugar and the melted margarine with fork in 13×9-inch baking pan until crumbs are well moistened. Press firmly onto bottom of pan to form crust. Refrigerate.

Orange Jack-O'-Lanterns

INGREDIENTS
6 oranges
1 package (5 ounces)
  cook-and-serve
  chocolate pudding
  mix
2¼ cups milk
1 cup mini semisweet
  chocolate chips
4 ounces cream cheese,
  softened and cut into
  ½-inch cubes
½ teaspoon orange extract
Green Cream Cheese
  Frosting (recipe
  follows)
Green Slivered Almonds
  (recipe follows)

SUPPLIES
Pastry bag with leaf tip

◆ Cut tops from oranges; discard tops. Scoop out fruit and membranes; reserve for another use or discard. With sharp knife, cut out jack-o'-lantern faces in sides of oranges.

◆ Combine pudding mix and milk in medium saucepan. Cook over medium-high heat, stirring constantly, until pudding comes to a boil. Remove saucepan from heat. Add chocolate chips, cream cheese and extract; stir until chips and cream cheese are melted. Cool.

◆ Spoon pudding mixture into oranges. Cover lightly with plastic wrap; refrigerate several hours or overnight.

◆ When ready to serve, spoon Green Cream Cheese Frosting into pastry bag fitted with leaf tip; pipe onto pudding for pumpkin leaves as shown in photo on page 105. Add almonds for stems, if desired.

Makes 6 servings

Green Cream Cheese Frosting

4 ounces cream cheese,
  softened
2 tablespoons powdered
  sugar
Green food color

◆ Beat cream cheese and powdered sugar in small bowl until well blended. Color with green food color.

Makes about ½ cup

Green Slivered Almonds: Place 6 slivered almonds in small resealable plastic food storage bag. Add ⅛ teaspoon green food color; seal bag. Shake bag until almonds are evenly colored. Place almonds on paper-towel-lined plate; let dry.

Smucker's®
Spider Web
Tartlets

1 16-ounce log
   refrigerated sugar
   cookie dough
¾ cup flour
   Nonstick cooking spray
   or parchment paper
1 cup (12-ounce jar)
   SMUCKER'S® Apricot
   Preserves
1 tube black cake
   decorating gel

◆ Preheat the oven to 375°F. Unwrap cookie dough and place in medium mixing bowl. With floured hands, knead flour into cookie dough. Roll dough back into log shape, place on clean cutting board and cut into eight equal slices. With floured fingers, place dough circles onto baking sheet lined with parchment paper or sprayed with nonstick spray.

◆ Gently press dough circles, flattening to make each one approximately 4 inches in diameter. With thumb and forefinger, pinch the edge of each dough circle to create a ridge all around. Pinch each dough circle along the ridge to make eight points.

◆ Spread 2 tablespoons of Smucker's® Preserves (or Simply Fruit) onto each dough circle, making sure to spread it all the way to the edges and in the points. Refrigerate for 20 minutes. Bake 12 to 14 minutes or until edges are lightly browned.

◆ Remove tartlets from baking sheet and cool on wire rack. When cool, use the black decorating gel to make a spider web design.   *Makes 8 servings*

For a really eerie setting, replace regular light bulbs with black, strobe or colored light bulbs. Then arrange false cobwebs on and around the lamp shades to create some menacing shadows.

Yummy Mummy Cookies

⅔ cup butter or
   margarine, softened
1 cup sugar
2 teaspoons vanilla
   extract
2 eggs
2½ cups all-purpose flour
½ cup HERSHEY'S Cocoa
¼ teaspoon baking soda
½ teaspoon salt
1 cup HERSHEY'S MINI
   CHIPS™ Semi-Sweet
   Chocolate
1 to 2 packages
   (10 ounces each)
   HERSHEY'S Premier
   White Chips
1 to 2 tablespoons
   shortening (do not
   use butter, margarine,
   spread or oil)
Additional HERSHEY'S
   MINI CHIPS™ Semi-
   Sweet Chocolate

1. Beat butter, sugar and vanilla in large bowl until creamy. Add eggs; beat well. Stir together flour, cocoa, baking soda and salt; gradually add to butter mixture, beating until blended. Stir in 1 cup small chocolate chips. Refrigerate dough 15 to 20 minutes or until firm enough to handle.

2. Heat oven to 350°F. To form mummy body, using 1 tablespoon dough, roll into 3½-inch carrot shape; place on ungreased cookie sheet. To form head, using 1 teaspoon dough, roll into ball the size and shape of a grape; press onto wide end of body. Repeat procedure with remaining dough. Bake 8 to 9 minutes or until set. Cool slightly; remove from cookie sheet to wire rack. Cool.

3. Place 1⅔ cups (10-ounce package) white chips and 1 tablespoon shortening in microwave-safe pie plate or shallow bowl. Microwave at HIGH (100%) 1 minute; stir until chips are melted.

4. Coat tops of cookies by placing one cookie at a time on table knife or narrow metal spatula; spoon white chip mixture evenly over cookie to coat. (If mixture begins to thicken, return to microwave for a few seconds). Place coated cookies on wax paper. Melt additional chips with shortening, if needed, for additional coating. As coating begins to set on cookies, using a toothpick, score lines and facial features into coating to resemble mummy. Place 2 small chocolate chips on each cookie for eyes. Store, covered, in cool, dry place.
Makes about 30 cookies

Yummy Mummy Cookies

Macho Monster Cake

1 package (18.25 ounces) cake mix, any flavor, plus ingredients to prepare mix
1 container (16 ounces) cream cheese or vanilla frosting
Green and yellow food color
Black decorating gel
1 white chocolate baking bar (2 ounces)

SUPPLIES
1 (13×9-inch) cake board, covered, or large tray

◆ Preheat oven to 350°F. Lightly grease and flour 13×9-inch baking pan.

◆ Prepare cake mix according to package directions. Pour into prepared pan.

◆ Bake 30 to 35 minutes until toothpick inserted into center comes out clean. Cool in pan on wire rack 10 minutes. Remove to rack; cool completely.

◆ Tint frosting with green and yellow food color to make ugly monster green as shown in photo. If cake top is rounded, trim horizontally with long serrated knife. Using Diagram 1 as guide, draw pattern pieces on waxed paper. Cut pieces out and place on cake. Cut around patterns with knife. Remove and discard patterns.

◆ Position pieces on prepared cake board as shown in Diagram 2, connecting with some frosting. Frost cake. Using decorating gel, pipe eyes, mouth, hair and scars as shown. Break white chocolate baking bar into irregular pieces; position inside mouth as teeth.

Makes 12 servings

Note: For cleaner cutting lines, place the cooled cake in the freezer for 30 to 45 minutes before cutting.

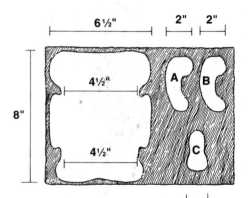

Diagram 1

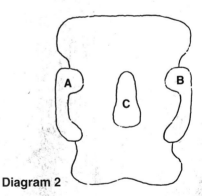

Diagram 2

Macho Monster Cake

Creepy Cookie Cauldrons

1 package (about
    18 ounces)
    refrigerated chocolate
    cookie dough*
All-purpose flour
1 bag (14 ounces)
    caramels, unwrapped
2 tablespoons milk
1 cup crisp rice cereal
¼ cup mini candy-coated
    chocolate pieces
Black licorice whips
    and small gummy
    insects, frogs or
    lizards

*If refrigerated chocolate cookie dough is unavailable, add ¼ cup unsweetened cocoa powder to refrigerated sugar cookie dough. Beat in large bowl until well blended.

◆ Grease 36 (1¾-inch) mini muffin cups. Remove dough from wrapper according to package directions. Sprinkle dough with flour to minimize sticking, if necessary.

◆ Cut dough into 36 equal pieces; roll into balls. Place 1 ball in bottom of each muffin cup. Press dough on bottoms and up sides of muffin cups; chill 15 minutes. Preheat oven to 350°F.

◆ Bake 8 to 9 minutes. (Cookies will be puffy.) Remove from oven; gently press down center of each cookie. Return to oven 1 minute. Cool cookies in muffin cups 5 minutes. Remove to wire racks; cool completely.

◆ Melt caramels and milk in small saucepan over low heat, stirring frequently until smooth. Stir in cereal. Spoon 1 heaping teaspoon caramel mixture into each cookie cup. Immediately sprinkle with mini chocolate pieces.

◆ Cut licorice whips into 4½-inch lengths. For each cookie, make small slit in side; insert end of licorice strip. Repeat on other side of cookie to make cauldron handle. Decorate with gummy creatures.

Makes 3 dozen cookies

Set a creepy table for your party! For each guest, roll up a paper napkin and use a plastic spider ring as a napkin ring.

Creepy Cookie Cauldrons

Halloween Haunted House

1 container (16 ounces) chocolate fudge frosting
Pretzel sticks, nuts, fudge-coated graham crackers, black licorice twists, black jelly beans, sugar wafers, candy corn, dried papaya, rice crackers, and other assorted candies

SUPPLIES
2 empty 1-quart milk cartons, rinsed and dried
1 (13×11-inch) cake board, covered, or large tray

◆ Tape each milk carton closed at top. Tape milk cartons together to make house; wrap with foil. Attach securely to covered cake board with tape.

◆ Frost cartons with chocolate frosting; decorate using frosting to attach decorations.

Makes 1 house

Chocolate Spiders

¼ cup butter
1 package (12 ounces) semisweet chocolate chips
1 cup butterscotch chips
¼ cup creamy peanut butter
4 cups crisp rice cereal
Chow mein noodles and assorted candies

◆ Cover baking sheet with waxed paper. Combine butter, chocolate chips and butterscotch chips in large saucepan; stir over medium heat until chips are melted and mixture is well blended. Remove from heat. Add peanut butter; mix well. Add cereal; stir to evenly coat.

◆ Drop mixture by tablespoonfuls onto prepared baking sheet; insert chow mein noodles for legs and add candies for eyes.   *Makes about 3 dozen*

Doughnut Hole Spiders:

Substitute chocolate-covered doughnut holes for shaped cereal mixture. Insert black string licorice, cut into 1½-inch lengths, into doughnut holes for legs. Use decorating icing to dot onto doughnut holes for eyes.

Halloween Haunted House

Patterns

Halloween Wreath

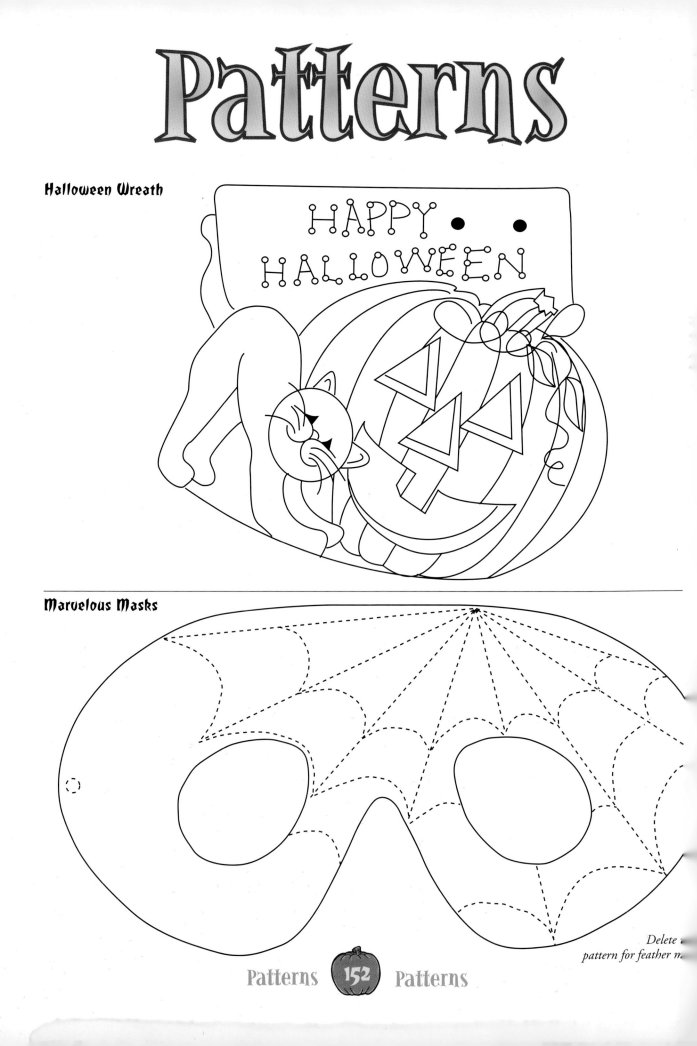

HAPPY HALLOWEEN

Marvelous Masks

*Delete
pattern for feather m*

Welcome Placard

Enlarge 130 percent

Trick or TREATERS Welcome

Halloween Button Covers

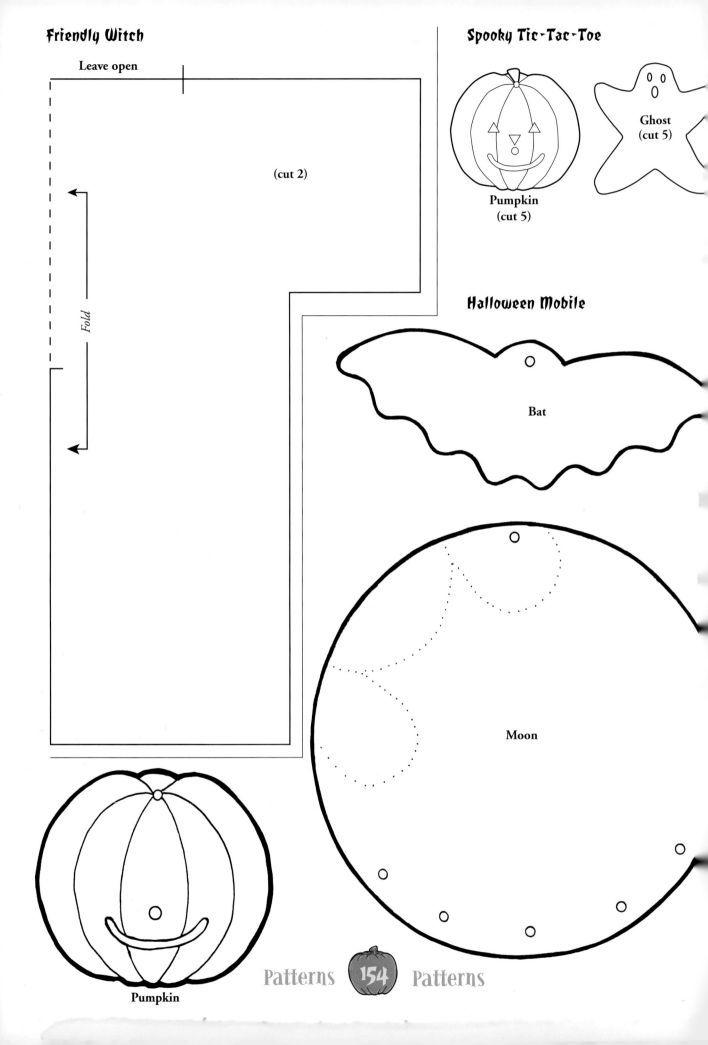

Friendly Witch

Leave open

Fold

(cut 2)

Pumpkin

Spooky Tic-Tac-Toe

Pumpkin
(cut 5)

Ghost
(cut 5)

Halloween Mobile

Bat

Moon

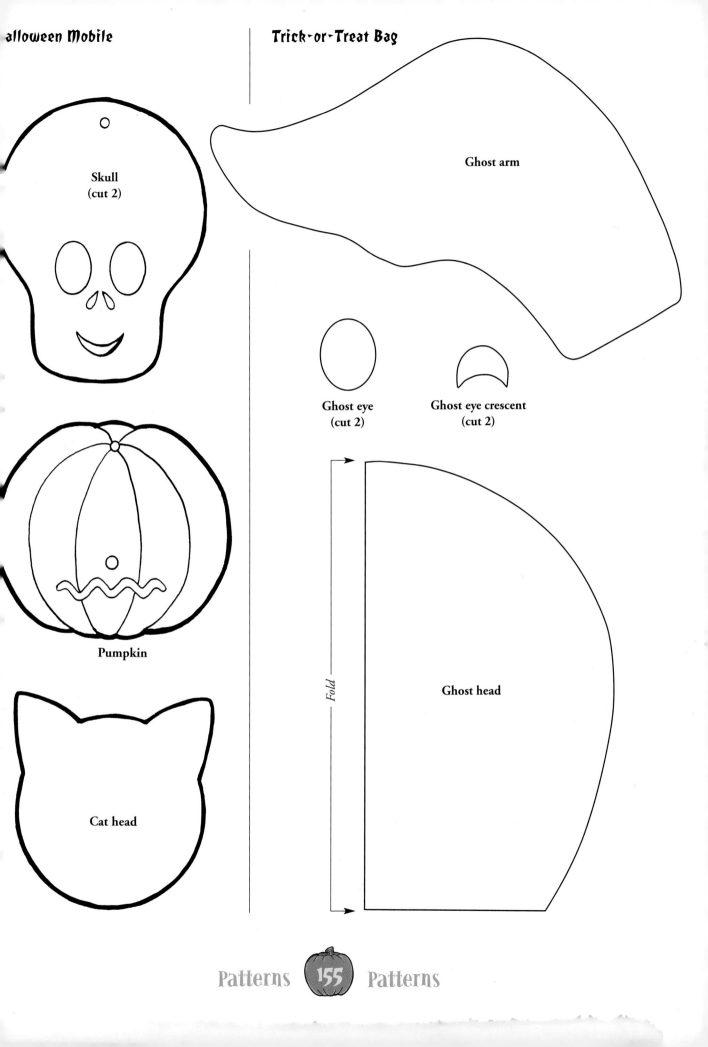

Skull
(cut 2)

Ghost arm

Ghost eye
(cut 2)

Ghost eye crescent
(cut 2)

Pumpkin

Fold

Ghost head

Cat head

Trick-or-Treat Bag

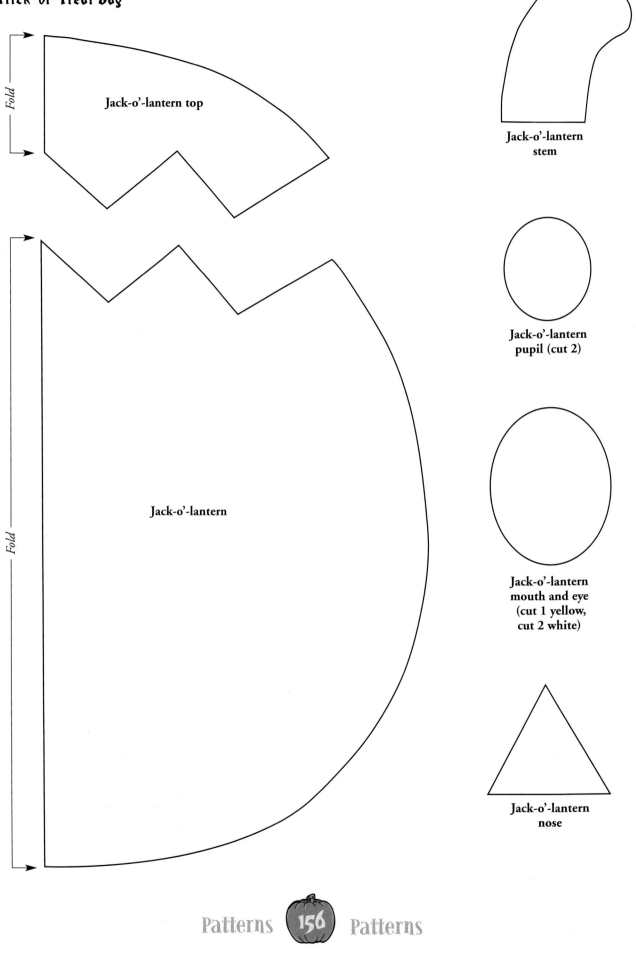

Fold

Jack-o'-lantern top

Fold

Jack-o'-lantern

Jack-o'-lantern
stem

Jack-o'-lantern
pupil (cut 2)

Jack-o'-lantern
mouth and eye
(cut 1 yellow,
cut 2 white)

Jack-o'-lantern
nose

rietta Witch

ge 200 percent

Head–body
(cut 2)

A

B

Back neck

Front neck

Fold

Vest
(cut 2)

Hat
(cut 1)

Attach sleeve

Dress
(cut 2)

Fold

Leg–shoe
(cut 4)

Arm
(cut 4)

Fold

Sleeve
(cut 2)

Index

Acknowledgments

The publisher would like to thank the companies and organizations listed below for the use of their recipes and photographs in this publication.

Birds Eye®
Hershey Foods Corporation
Idaho Potato Commission
Kraft Foods Holdings
Lipton®
Nabisco Biscuit Company
National Chicken Council
PLANTERS® Baking Nuts
The J.M. Smucker Company
Washington Apple Commission